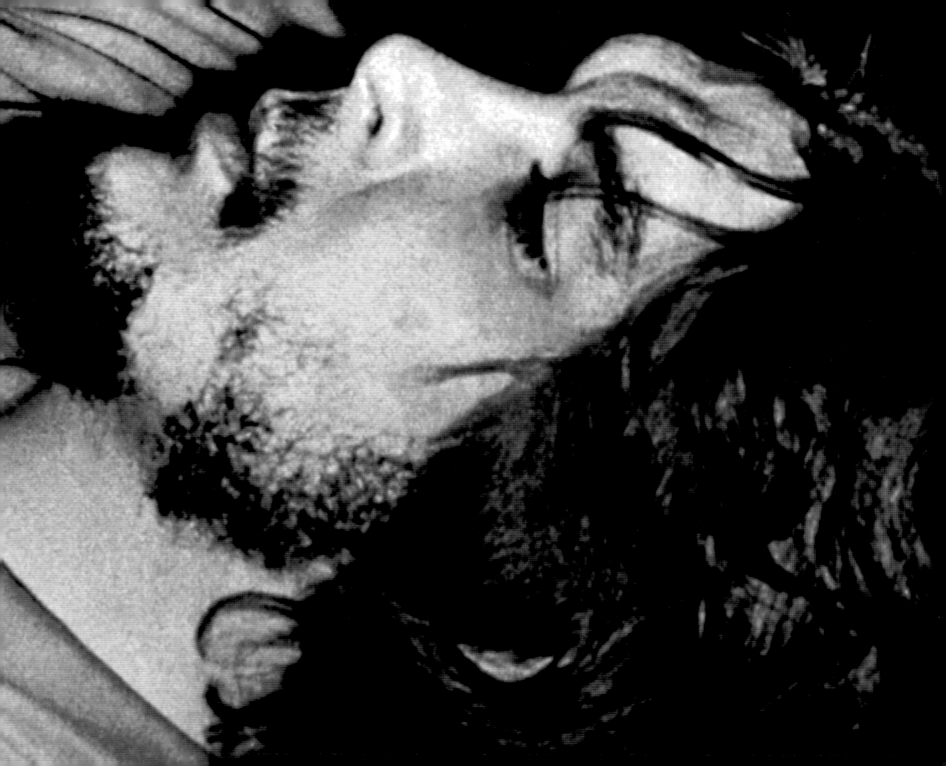

self portrait che guevara

ERNESTO CHE GUEVARA

self portrait
che guevara

ERNESTO CHE GUEVARA

Edited by Víctor Casaus

Centro de Estudios
CHE GUEVARA

ocean

Cover and Internal Design by **::maybe**
Al Briggs, Velco Dojcinovski and Steve White
www.maybe.com.au

Copyright © 2004 Ocean Press
Copyright © 2004 Che Guevara Studies Center and Aleida March
All Photographs Copyright © Che Guevara Studies Center and Aleida March

ISBN 1-876175-82-6
Library of Congress Control No: 2004100386
First Printed in 2004

Published by Ocean Press
Australia: GPO Box 3279, Melbourne, Victoria 3001, Australia
    Tel: (61-3) 9326 4280 Fax: (61-3) 9329 5040
    E-mail: info@oceanbooks.com.au

USA: PO Box 1186, Old Chelsea Stn., New York, NY 10113-1186, USA

Ocean Press Distributors:
United States and Canada: **Consortium Book Sales and Distribution**
Tel: 1-800-283-3572 www.cbsd.com

Australia and New Zealand: **Palgrave Macmillan**
E-mail: customer.service@macmillan.com.au

Britain and Europe: **Pluto Books**
E-mail: pluto@plutobooks.com

Cuba and Latin America: **Ocean Press**
E-mail: oceanhav@enet.cu

www.oceanbooks.com.au
info@oceanbooks.com.au

ernesto che guevara

One of *Time* magazine's "icons of the century," Ernesto Guevara de la Serna was born in Rosario, Argentina, on June 14, 1928. He made several trips around Latin America during and immediately after his studies at medical school in Buenos Aires, including his 1952 journey with Alberto Granado, on the unreliable Norton motorbike described in his travel journal *The Motorcycle Diaries*.

He was already becoming involved in political activity and living in Guatemala when, in 1954, the elected government of Jacobo Arbenz was overthrown in a CIA-organized military operation. Ernesto escaped to Mexico, profoundly radicalized.

Following up on a contact made in Guatemala, Guevara sought out the group of exiled Cuban revolutionaries in Mexico City. In July 1955, he met Fidel Castro and immediately enlisted in the guerrilla expedition to overthrow Cuban dictator Fulgencio Batista. The Cubans nicknamed him "Che," a popular form of address in Argentina.

On November 25, 1956, Guevara set sail for Cuba aboard the yacht *Gramma* as the doctor to the guerrilla group that began the revolutionary armed struggle in Cuba's Sierra Maestra

mountains. Within several months, he became the first Rebel Army commander, though he continued to attend to wounded guerrilla fighters and captured soldiers from Batista's army.

In September 1958, Guevara played a decisive role in the military defeat of Batista after he and Camilo Cienfuegos led separate guerrilla columns westward from the Sierra Maestra.

After Batista fled on January 1, 1959, Guevara became a key leader of the new revolutionary government, first as head of the Industrial Department of the National Institute of Agrarian Reform; then as president of the National Bank. In February 1961 he became minister of industry. He was also a central leader of the political organization that in 1965 became the Communist Party of Cuba.

Apart from these responsibilities, Guevara represented the Cuban revolutionary government around the world, heading numerous delegations and speaking at the United Nations and other international forums in Asia, Africa, Latin America and the socialist bloc countries. He earned a reputation as a passionate and articulate spokesperson for Third

World peoples, most famously at the conference at Punta del Este in Uruguay, where he denounced U.S. President Kennedy's Alliance for Progress.

As had been his intention since joining the Cuban revolutionary movement, Guevara left Cuba in April 1965, initially to lead a guerrilla mission to support the revolutionary struggle in the Congo. He returned to Cuba secretly in December 1965, to prepare another guerrilla force for Bolivia. Arriving in Bolivia in November 1966, Guevara's plan was to challenge that country's military dictatorship and eventually to instigate a revolutionary movement that would extend throughout the continent of Latin America. He was wounded and captured by U.S.-trained and run Bolivian counterinsurgency troops on October 8, 1967. The following day he was murdered and his body hidden.

Che Guevara's remains were finally discovered in 1997 and returned to Cuba. A memorial was built at Santa Clara in central Cuba, where he had won a major military battle during the revolutionary war.

contents

prologue

05. chronicles from the sierra maestra

06. behind the lens

07. fielding questions

to begin, continue

Che The Witness is another title we might have given this book, in order to highlight the other calling — lesser known but equally rich — running through the life, journeys and deeds of Ernesto Che Guevara de la Serna, from his restless youth to his formidable adulthood. It is almost unnerving to see how systematically he plied this trade and, indeed, incorporated it into his existence. In this book, which follows the trail of his research, his dreams, his battles and his challenges, appear examples of his vocation as a witness: his travel diaries, letters, interviews, journalism and photos.

The text has been ordered more or less chronologically so that it is possible to explore, from letter to letter, note to note, Che's pursuit of this calling, the development of his ideas and fundamental convictions. In this sense, the book, too, bears witness.

It bears witness to the "Guevara ethic" applied to literary creation. "I believe that writing is a way of facing up to concrete problems, a position one adopts toward life because of one's sensitivity," he responds in a letter written in the 1960s, bringing together two significant elements of his own experience: practical action and human and artistic sensibility. In another letter from the same period he replies to a writer, "the only passion that guides me in this field of yours is conveying the truth (and do not take me here for a hard-line defender of socialist realism). I look at everything from this point of view." The bracketed words — like those reflections in his essay "Socialism and Man in Cuba" — reveal to us yet again the intellectual formed and informed by the issues that attract his attention and occupy his time.

Like any of those that bear real witness, the text in this book reveals different aspects of the author's personality. We find him in these pages as a reader and photographer, a friend and historian, a man who studied people and life. Irony, humor, criticism, strength, sincerity and demanding self-scrutiny come

together in Che's observant words. Here they appear just as they were, as they are, doing justice to his statement that is rich with lessons for both present and future: "I consider that historical truth must be respected; capricious invention cannot lead to anything good."

Che was a conspirator in defense of this truth, laboring against overwhelming injustice and paralyzing dogma from the standpoint of history and the true word.

It is therefore an honor for the Pablo de la Torriente Brau Cultural Center — a space for memory and debate, imagination and beauty — to have been able to work with the Che Guevara Studies Center and Ocean Press in the first real attempt to explore this theme, based on an issue of the magazine *Memoria* which we jointly produced in 1997.

That project, both idealistic and practical, grew into this book. It has been produced with rigor and love, in tune with Che's times, in order to show, in our own uncertain times,

the cutting edge of this multifaceted and creative personality. Che used ethics as weapon in his struggle to create a world where this new ethic would be possible, something we could take for granted, something that would be ours.

This is a book for all those young people, in whatever corner of the planet they may be, who question the world of today as the youthful Ernesto did, a world becoming increasingly incomprehensible, out of reach and unjust.

By defending intelligence, solidarity and justice, the following pages attempt to bring this cultured, incisive, ironic, passionate and worldly Che — the living Che — closer to us all.

I shall leave you then, with *el que fue* (the man that used to be), with the man that is, and with the man that — if we all come together to make it possible — will be.

Victor Casaus
Havana

n inveterate traveler, a seeker of landscape, vocation and destiny, Ernesto Guevara was already the Che of the triumphant Cuban Revolution when someone asked him about his family's origins. In this memorable letter written early in 1964, Che responds to a distant, imagined relative, and reaffirms his position on this topic.

We now begin the journey of this book, tracing Che's footsteps and discoveries, reliving his questions and his growing responses. This letter accompanies photographs of Ernesto, starting from his childhood and his personal challenges, following him through education and combat to maturity.

It is more than a family chronicle, more than an enumeration of dates and places. This brief, direct letter, almost certainly written in a moment snatched between other commitments, reveals Che's most profound concept of the human family.

—VC

if you are capable of
trembling with
indignation...

...our
imagination.

Havana, February 20, 1964
"Year of the Economy"

Sra. María Rosario Guevara

36, rue d'Annam

(Maarif) Casablanca

Morocco

Compañera,

Truthfully speaking, I don't know what part of Spain my family came from. Of course, considerable time has passed since my forbears left there, with one hand in front and another behind;* and if I don't keep mine in the same place, it is only because of the discomfort of the position.

I don't think you and I are very closely related, but if you are capable of trembling with indignation each time an injustice is committed in the world, we are comrades, and that is more important.

A revolutionary greeting,

"Patria o muerte. Venceremos."

Comandante Ernesto Che Guevara

* A saying in Spanish indicating severe poverty.

These pages: Early infancy with Celia and Ernesto, his parents, 1929.

Following pages: Childhood days on the family swing.

Above: On one of his many Rocinantes. Altagracia, Córdoba, Argentina.
Below and Left: Altagracia, Córdoba, Argentina.

Above: Altagracia, Córdoba, Argentina.

Below: With his family in Mar del Plata, Argentina.
Right: With "Chichina" Ferreira. Córdoba, Argentina, 1950.

As a student, from Buenos Aires
to Córdoba, Argentina, 1951.
Right: As a doctor.

H ere, the young Ernesto begins his travels; he is seeing Argentina from within, yet beyond Buenos Aires, Rosario and Córdoba. Here, are fragments of his journeying through dusty Santiago del Estero to Salta, where the Juramento River invites him with its "gray foam leaping like sparks as the water crashed against the rocks [to] plunge in, to be rocked brutally by its waters," leaving him with a desire "to shout like mad without any regard for what one was saying."

His encounter with nature in the north of Argentina, described in beautiful, precise and clear prose, shot through with ironic and dazzling flashes, goes hand in hand with his particular way of seeing things: this young witness looks beyond the deceptive appearance of "the plush covering" in the "tourist maps of Jujuy," to find the spirit of the region and its inhabitants. It is a gaze which expands with time, along the paths he will trace and retrace, approaching the horizons of the planet and the people who inhabit it.

This trip marks the start of the young Ernesto's contact with a world beyond the narrow confines of family. His search for adventure and unknown places is accompanied by a personal challenge: the struggle to gain control over his asthma and in testing his will on the road.

The traveler discovers utterly new aspects of nature and begins to perceive — with a clarity that never ceases to sharpen — the nuances of human society in the world opening up before his eyes. In this process, there is nothing like knowledge of the other, the exchanges of an unexpected conversation:

"...a tramp appeared, sheltering under a small bridge, and naturally we began to talk. This man had been picking cotton in Chaco and, after wandering about for a while, was thinking of heading for the grape harvest in San Juan... When he learned of my plan to travel through several provinces, and discovered that my exploits were nothing more than a joyride, he clasped his head in despair: 'Mamma mia, you're putting all this effort into nothing?...'"

—VC

inside argentina

2

theimpetuous attempt...

This is a retrospective view of some aspects prior to my first journey, which initially was meant to take in only two or three parts of the province of Córdoba, yet which grew into the impetuous attempt to reach Santiago, Tucumán, Catamarca, La Rioja, San Juan, Mendoza, San Luis, Buenos Aires and Miramar.

Right: Buenos Aires, Argentina, 1951.

i laughed at the downpour...

When I left Buenos Aires on the night of January 1, 1950, I was full of doubts about the potential of my bike's motor and my only hope was of reaching Pilar quickly and in one piece (the end of my journey according to some well-intentioned tongues at home), and then going on to Pergamino, another of the final destinations they set for me.

As I left San Isidro and rode along the track, I shut down the little motor and pedaled onwards, so that another rider, traveling to Rosario by leg-power (on his bicycle) caught up with me. We continued together, me pedaling to keep the same speed as my companion. As I passed through Pilar, I felt the first joys of victory.

At eight the following morning, we reached the first stage in my companion's journey, San Antonio de Areco, where we breakfasted together and said our goodbyes. I continued along my way and reached Pergamino by nightfall. At this second, symbolic stage I was so triumphant and emboldened by success that I forgot my fatigue and set off toward Rosario, hanging honorably on to a fuel truck, reaching Rosario by 11 that night. My body was screaming for a mattress, but my will won out and I continued. At around two in the morning there was a cloudburst that lasted about an hour. I took out my raincoat and the sailcloth cape that had found its way into my pack through my foresight, laughed at the downpour and burbled a verse of Sábato at the top of my lungs…

At six in the morning I arrived in Leones, changed the spark plugs and filled the tank. The ride now moved into a monotonous stretch. At about 10 in the morning I went through Belle Ville and attached myself to the back of another truck that towed me close to Villa María, where I stopped a moment to do some calculations, according to which I had taken less than 40 hours to get there. I had 144 kilometers to go, at 25 kilometers per hour, so there was nothing more to say. After another 10 kilometers along the track, a private car caught up with me — I was pedaling then to avoid overheating the motor in the midday sun — and stopped to see if I needed fuel. I said I didn't but asked if he could tow me along at 60 kilometers per hour. I'd done 10 kilometers when the back tire burst and, caught off guard, my entire humanity bit the dust* (a wonderful view of the ground with one's face in the road).

Investigating the cause of the disaster, I found that the motor, running unnecessarily, had eaten through the tire, exposing the inner tube and causing my fall.

With no spares and terribly tired, I flung myself down by the road to rest. After an hour or two, an empty truck came along and the driver agreed to take me to Córdoba. I packed my… things in a hire car and got to Granado, the goal of my labors, in a total of 41 hours 17 minutes… In the [illegible] I have already written about, I met up with a tramp who was napping under a little bridge

and who woke with the commotion. We started to talk, and when he learned that I was a student he took a liking to me. He brought out a dirty thermos and made me *mate* with enough sugar to sweeten up any spinster. After a long chat, describing our various adventures to each other, embellishing to be sure but perhaps with some truth, he remembered his days as a barber and, noting my rather long locks, took out some rusty scissors and a dirty comb and set about the job. Halfway through, I felt something strange happening to my head and began to fear for my physical safety, but I never imagined that a pair of scissors could be such a dangerous weapon. When he offered a small mirror that he took from his pocket, I nearly fell over — he'd cut so many different layers that not a patch on my head was left undamaged.

I carried my shorn head like a kind of trophy to the Aguilar house when I went to visit my sister Ana María. To my surprise they attached scant importance to the shearing, but were amazed I had drunk the *mate* he had given me. Regarding these opinions nothing has been written.

After a few days of rest waiting for Tomasito, we left for Tanti. The place we were headed to was nothing out of the ordinary, but was near facilities including fresh spring water. After two days, we headed off on our planned journey to Los Chorrillos, some 10 kilometers away.

The vision of the Los Chorrillos waterfall from a height of some 50 meters is something really worth seeing in the Córdoba ranges. As the water falls, it separates into multiple small streams that ricochet off every stone until they scatter and fall into a lower basin and then, in a profusion of lesser falls, into a large natural basin. It is the biggest I have seen in streams of this size, but unfortunately it gets very little sunlight, so the water is extremely cold and one can only stay in a few minutes.

The abundance of water on all the surrounding slopes, emerging from natural springs, makes this place extremely fertile and there is an explosion of ferns and other damp-loving plants, lending a spectacular beauty to this place.

In this area, above the waterfall, I first tried rock climbing. I had got it into my head to descend where the waterfall trickled gently down, but for more thrills I chose a hazardous short cut, the most difficult I could find.

Halfway down, a stone came loose and amid an avalanche of stones and loose rocks, I fell some 10 meters.

When I finally managed to find my footing, after breaking several [illegible], I had to start climbing up because it was impossible to descend further. Here I learned the first law of rock climbing: going up is easier than going down. The bitter taste of defeat stayed with me all day, but the next day I dived from four meters, or (at least) two meters, into 70 centimeters of water. Wiping out the bitter taste of the previous day.

That day and part of the next it rained a lot… and we decided to pack up the tent. At around 5:30, as we were sluggishly gathering our bits and pieces together… came the first throaty roar of the torrent. People spilled out of the neighboring houses, all yelling, "The water's coming down, the water's coming down!" Our whole camp was awash with people, the three of us running back and forth with our things. At the last minute, "El Grego" Granado picked up one of the corners of the tent cover, sweeping away all that remained, while Tomás and I pulled out the pegs at full speed. The flood was visibly bearing down on us and the people nearby were shouting, "Leave it, you madmen!" plus a few other fairly unCatholic words. But at that point, only one rope was left. I had the machete in my hand and lost control. While everyone watched with baited breath, I shouted, "Charge, brave "men!" and, with a theatrical blow, cut the tether. We were still getting everything to one side when the torrent came down, roaring furiously and revealing itself in all its incredible height — one and a half meters — amid interminable deafening noise.

I left at four in the afternoon on January 29, and, after a short stop in Colonia Caroya, headed for San José de la Dormida,** where I paid homage to the name of the place by lying down by the side of the road; I had a magnificent night's sleep until six the following morning.

I pedaled about five kilometers further until I found a little house where they sold me a liter of fuel.

On the final stretch to San Francisco del Chañar, I started out in second. The little motor decided to take fright on a steep climb and left me to pedal about five kilometers, all uphill, but finally I found myself in the middle of the village. The van from the leprosy sanatorium gave me a lift from there.

The next day, we visited one of Alberto Granado's [illegible] with a Doctor Rosetti. On the way back I fell off the bike, snapping eight spokes, leaving me stranded four days longer than planned until they fixed it...

We'd planned to leave on the Saturday... with Alberto Granado, after a party or at least a drink at Mr. X's place, this man being senator for the region, the local head honcho, a modern lord of the knife and noose...

We spent the whole morning debating how to get away quickly. Finally, early in the afternoon, we decided to leave, me on the bike and [Alberto] and a friend on the motorbike. But first, we had determined to have a glass of their vermouth, which was something special... There was no ice, so the little fellow went off to get some but couldn't find any. I was getting upset, so he went to ask for a bag of ice at the senator's house, brought it back and we set about the vermouth with unusual zeal. As bad luck would have it, the senator's wife suddenly remembered that she needed some "medicine" and came to find it. When we noticed her august presence it was already too late but, in any case, I flung myself down on the mattress, holding my head desperately as if in pain, only doing so to show off my gifts as an actor because I already knew that it was in vain...

* An Argentine phrase meaning to fall from a vehicle or horse.

** Sleep or overnight stop.

santiagodelestero: thesunbeatdown onmyhead...

This part of the Santiago landscape reminds me of some areas to the north of Córdoba, from which it is separated only by an imaginary line. Along the sides of the roads there are enormous cacti, some six meters tall, like giant green candelabras. The vegetation is abundant and there are signs of fertile life, but the scene slowly changes, the road becomes rough and dusty, the quebracho trees disappear and starwort shows signs of taking over.

The sun beat down on my head, enveloping me in waves of heat as I bumped over the ground. I chose the leafy shade of a carob tree and lay down to sleep for an hour, got up, had a couple of *mates* and got on with the journey. Along the track, the milestone on Route 9 marking kilometer 1,000 welcomed me. One kilometer later, the starwort took over completely and I was now in the Sahara but, suddenly and to my great surprise, the track (privileged to be one of the worst so far), turned into a magnificently sealed, firm, flat path where the motor was in its element, ticking over happily.

This was not the only surprise that the heartland of the republic had in store for me — the fact of coming upon a ranch every four or five kilometers made me wonder whether I really was in this tragic place at all. But the ocean of silver-stained earth and its green mane allowed no room for doubt. At intervals, like a sprawling sentinel, the vigilant figure of a cactus appeared.

In two-and-a-half hours I covered 80 kilometers of salt pan and then I got another surprise: when I asked for some cool water to replace what had been warming up in my water bottle I learned that there was plenty of drinking water only three meters below the ground. Evidently, reputation is subordinate to subjective impression, unless there is some other explanation for the following phenomena: good roads, a lot of ranches, water at three meters. It is no small thing.

After nightfall I came to Loreto, a town of several thousand souls, but still very backward.

The police officer I saw when I went to ask about somewhere to spend the night told me there was not a single doctor in the town and, when he learned that I was doing fifth-year medicine, gave me the sound advice that I should set myself up there as the town healer. "They earn a lot of money and do us a favor, too"...

But I set off early, moving along some stretches of HORRIBLE track and others with very good surfaces. I parted ways forever with my water bottle which was claimed by a treacherous pothole, and eventually reached Santiago where I was given a warm reception by a family I know there.

It was here that the first report about me was done for a Tucumán newspaper, written by a Señor Santillan, who met me on my first call in the town...

That day I discovered the city of Santiago... where the infernal heat is too much even for its inhabitants, who remain locked at home until the evening, when they come out into the streets to get on with their social life.

tucumán: while i stopped to inflate a tire...

At nine in the morning the next day I continued on my way to Tucumán where I arrived late that night.

At one point along the way something curious happened while I stopped to inflate a tire, about a thousand meters out from a town. A tramp appeared, sheltering under a small bridge, and naturally we began to talk. This man had been picking cotton in Chaco and, after wandering about for a while, was thinking of heading for the grape harvest in San Juan... When he learned of my plan to travel through several provinces, and discovered that my exploits were nothing more than a joyride, he clasped his head in despair: "Mamma mia, you're putting all this effort into nothing?" ...

I set off again toward the capital of Tucumán province. Like a flash, I flitted through the majestic town of Tucumán at 30 miles an hour and immediately took the road to Salta, but was surprised by rain so I humbly ended up in the armory of a barracks, from where I left for Salta at six in the morning.

On the road out of Tucumán is one of the most beautiful sights in the north [of Argentina]. Along some

20 kilometers of good road is lush vegetation on both sides, a kind of tropical forest within the tourist's reach, with a million little streams and a humid atmosphere that makes the place seem like a film set of the Amazon jungle. Entering these natural gardens, walking among the lianas, treading through the ferns, observing how everything here makes fun of our scant botanic culture, one expects every moment to hear a lion roar, to see a snake glide silently by or the agile movement of a deer. Suddenly there was a roar, not very loud though constant, but it turned out to be the chugging of a truck laboring up the slope.

This clamorous roar smashed the glass castle of my reverie, bringing me back to reality. I realized then that something which had been growing in me for some time, in the hustle and bustle of the city, was now mature: a hatred of civilization. The crude sight of people rushing about like mad things, to the beat of a tremendous noise, now seemed to me the loathsome antithesis of peace, of this [illegible] which formed a harmonious background music in the quiet rustling of the leaves.

I returned to the road and continued along my way. At 11 or 12 I came to a roadside police checkpoint and stopped to rest. Along came a motorcyclist on a brand new Harley Davidson and offered me a tow. I asked how fast. "If I go slow, about 80 or 90." But naturally I had learned from experience, at the cost of my ribs, that I can't go over 40 kilometers an hour while being towed, what with the instability of my load and the uneven roads.

I declined and after thanking [crossed out] who had invited me to a mug of coffee, I kept going, hoping to reach Salta in daylight. I had 200 kilometers still to go so I needed to get a move on.

At Rosario de la Frontera, I had an unhappy encounter at the police station. They were bringing the Harley Davidson off the back of a truck. I went over and asked about the rider. Dead, they said.

Naturally, the small, individual problem represented by the obscure death of this motorcyclist is not serious enough to affect the concerns or the sensibilities of the masses, but the knowledge that a man goes seeking danger without even the vague heroism associated with public exploits, and dies taking a bend without anyone to witness it, made this unknown adventurer seem to have some kind of ill-defined suicidal "fervor." It is something that might make the study of his personality interesting, but it completely removes him from the scope of these notes...

I presented myself at the hospital... as a "tired, half-adventurer, half-broke medical student." They offered me a station wagon with soft seats as lodgings, making a bed fit for a king. I slept like a log until seven in the morning when they woke me so they could use the car. The rain was torrential so my journey was delayed. At about two in the afternoon I headed off for Jujuy, but the road out of the city was boggy from the heavy downpour and it was impossible for me to go on. Nevertheless, I found a truck and it turned out that the driver was an old acquaintance. A few kilometers on, we went our separate ways, he to Campo Santo to collect cement while I headed off on a road known as La Cornisa.

The water that had fallen came together in little streams that descended from the surrounding hills and crossed the road to join the Mojotoro River, which runs alongside the road. This was not the impressive spectacle of Salta and the Juramento, but its cheerful beauty was a tonic for the spirit. After leaving the river behind, the traveler moves into the true regions of La Cornisa — its majestic beauty found in its hills adorned with green forest. There is one mountain pass after another, framed by the adjacent greenery. Through the branches, we saw the distant green plain as if through a tinted lens.

The wet foliage imbues the atmosphere with its cool and instead of the penetrating, aggressive humidity of Tucumán, there is something fresh and mild here. The charm of this warm, damp afternoon, refreshed by the dense forest... transported me to a dream world, a world very different from my present situation, but I knew the way back from it well. It was not cut off by the fog-filled abysses that the kingdoms of the good tend to flaunt...

Weary of so much beauty, like suffering indigestion from an excess of chocolate, I reached the town of Jujuy, with aches and pains inside and out, wanting to discover the measure of the province's hospitality. What better occasion than now to research the hospitals of the country?

I slept magnificently in one of the wards, but was first obliged to demonstrate my medical knowledge. Equipped with some tweezers and a bit of ether, I set about the thrilling hunt for [illegible] in a little kid's shaven head.

His monotonous whining lacerated my ears like a fine stiletto blade, while my other scientific self counted with indolent rapacity the number of my [dead] enemies. I can't understand how this little dark-skinned kid, barely two years old, could come to be so full of maggots. Even if you tried, it would not be easy to do...

I got into bed and tried to make of this insignificant episode a solid foundation for my pariah's sleep...

the biggest nanny goat in the herd chuckled at my clumsiness...

From Rosario de la Frontera to Metán the sealed and smooth road offered me a restful ride, preparing me for the stretch from Metán to Salta, which required a good dose of patience to [spot] the "serrations."

Nevertheless, no matter how bad this area is with respect to the roads, it was compensated for by the magnificent views it brandished. We came into a completely mountainous zone and, with each bend, there was something new to marvel at. Approaching Lobería, I was lucky to see one of the most beautiful scenes of my travels so far: at the edge of the road there was a kind of suspended railway bridge with the Juramento River running beneath. The banks are formed with stones of all colors and the river's gray waters chart their turbulent course through sheer cliffs covered in magnificent vegetation. I stayed a while looking at the water. In the gray foam, leaping like sparks

as the water crashed against the rocks and returned to the whirlpool, was the invitation to plunge in, to be rocked brutally by its waters, with a desire to shout like mad without any regard for what one was saying.

I climbed the slope feeling slightly melancholy; the roaring waters I was leaving behind seemed to reproach me for my romantic shortcomings, and I felt like a hardened bachelor. Above me and my philosophical, Jack London style beard, the biggest nanny goat in the herd chuckled at my clumsiness as a climber. Once again a truck's rasping groan dragged me out of my hermetic meditation.

After nightfall, I climbed the last hill and found before me the magnificent town of Salta. Its only weak point worthy of note is the fact that the tourist is welcomed by the geometric rigidity of the cemetery.

Right: With his uncle at the El Palomar airfield.

jujuy:no,onedoes notgettoknow atownlikethis...

I arrived in Salta at two in the afternoon, and went to visit some friends from the hospital. They were amazed to find I had done the whole trip in only one day, and so one of them asked, "But what do you see?" The question remains unanswered because it was formulated in such a way for there to be no answer. And that's the whole point, the real question: what *do* I see. I don't nourish myself on the same substance as other tourists, and I find it strange to see on tourist maps, Jujuy's for example, the Altar de la Patria, the cathedral where the national flag was blessed, the jewel of the pulpit and miraculous little virgin of Río Blanco and Pompeya, the house where Lavalle died, the city council of the revolution, the provincial museum, etc.

No, one does not get to know a town like this, to understand its interpretation of life or its way of living. All I have mentioned above is simply a plush covering, but its spirit is reflected in the patients of the hospitals, the inmates at the police station and the anxious pedestrian one chats to while the Río Grande displays its turbulent, swollen waters below. But all this takes a long time to explain and who knows if I would be understood. I gave thanks and set about discovering a town that I did not know very well when I left.

t the beginning of *The Motorcycle Diaries*, the young chronicler Ernesto Guevara proposes, "so we understand each other." And at that point he warns us that "the person who wrote these notes passed away the minute his feet touched Argentine soil. The person who reorganizes and polishes them, me, is no longer; at least, I'm not the person I once was." In this way he tells us that his vision has been changed, his analysis deepened, his spirit enriched by that "wandering around 'Our America with a capital A.'"

Che was only 23 when he began the journey, accompanied by his friend Alberto Granado. He left Argentina to see the world, to contemplate landscapes and continue looking beyond the horizon of his passion and the infinite curiosity of his youth. He had a feeling about a final return to his native land, and announced it then just as it would form part of his libertarian plans 15 years later: "Perhaps one day, tired of circling the world, I'll return to Argentina and settle on the Andean lakes, if not indefinitely then at least for a pause while I shift from one understanding of the world to another."

The fragments in this book unite some of the keys to understanding Che's first gaze at Latin America, "Our America with a capital A": the astonished discovery of pre-Columbian civilizations; the self-directed irony in the Chaplinesque episode of the Chilean puma; the continuation of his social and human apprenticeship in the passage about La Gioconda; the celebration of another year of his life, now on Peruvian soil, when he declares that "the division of America into unstable and illusory nations is completely fictional."

There is no doubting the passion and perseverance of Ernesto the chronicler, who reveals in his *Motorcycle Diaries* the testimonial style and the awareness of the undertaking he would subsequently make his own.

In this endless journey, various characteristics of the young man who would fulfill that role were sometimes imperceptibly being formed. Seen from the infallible perspective of the future, Ernesto's entire life appears to have been just that: one long journey of growth and dedication, of search and combat, of challenge and discovery, of analysis and reaffirmation.

The writer, concealed by the traveler, is also forged in this journey. The invaluable discoveries of real life were added to Ernesto's book-learned wisdom. Che the witness — a role he would play for the rest of his life — explores and narrates for us the realms of mystery, as in his "A note in the margin."

This undated chapter, here marking the chronological end to Ernesto's journey, captures the questions and uncertainties which overshadow humankind at the beginning of the 21st century. In this chronicle there are many threads to unravel, as we observe a new turn in the spiral of the traveler. After listening to the words of that man, full of light and shadow, Ernesto makes his premonition:

"The night, folding in at contact with his words, overtook me again, enveloping me within it. But despite his words, I now knew... I knew that when the great guiding spirit cleaves humanity into two antagonistic halves, I would be with the people..."

—VC

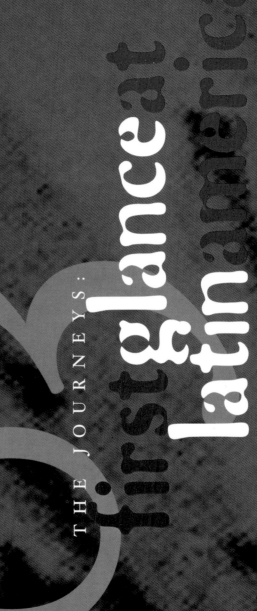

THE JOURNEYS:

first glance at
latin america

soweunderstandeachother

This is not a story of incredible heroism, or merely the narrative of a cynic; at least I do not mean it to be. It is a glimpse of two lives that ran parallel for a time, with similar hopes and convergent dreams.

In nine months of a man's life he can think a lot of things, from the loftiest meditations on philosophy to the most desperate longing for a bowl of soup — in total accord with the state of his stomach. And if, at the same time, he's somewhat of an adventurer, he might live through episodes of interest to other people and his haphazard record might read something like these notes.

And so, the coin was thrown in the air, turning many times, landing sometimes heads and other times tails. Man, the measure of all things, speaks here through my mouth and narrates in my own language that which my eyes have seen.

It is likely that out of 10 possible heads I have seen only one true tail, or vice versa. In fact it's probable, and there are no excuses, for these lips can only describe what these eyes actually see. Is it that our whole vision was never quite complete, that it was too transient or not always well-informed? Were we too uncompromising in our judgments? Okay, but this is how the typewriter interpreted those fleeting impulses raising my fingers to the keys, and those impulses have now died. Moreover, no one can be held responsible for them.

The person who wrote these notes passed away the moment his feet touched Argentine soil. The person who reorganizes and polishes them, me, is no longer; at least I'm not the person I once was. All this wandering around "Our America with a capital A" has changed me more than I thought.

In any photographic manual you'll come across the strikingly clear image of a landscape, apparently taken by night, in the light of a full moon. The secret behind this magical vision of "darkness at noon" is usually revealed in the accompanying text. Readers of this book will not be well versed about the sensitivity of my retina — I can hardly sense it myself. So they will not be able to check what is said against a photographic plate to discover at precisely what time each of my "pictures" was taken. What this means is that if I present you with an image and say, for instance, that it was taken at night, you can either believe me, or not; it matters little to me, since if you don't happen to know the scene I've "photographed" in my notes, it will be hard for you to find an alternative to the truth I'm about to tell. But I'll leave you now, with myself, the man I used to be...

Right: From Ernesto Guevara's original manuscript of *The Motorcycle Diaries*.

No es este el relato de hazañas impresionantes,no es tampoco mera-
mente un"relato un poco cínico"; no quiere serlo,por lo menos. Es un pedazo
de dos vidas tomadas en un momento en que cursaron juntas un determinado tre-
cho, juntxxxxix con identidad de aspiraciones y conjunción de sueños. Un hombre
en nueve meses de su vida puede pensar en muchas cosas que van de la más ele-
vada especulación filosófica al rastrero anhelo de un plato de sopa,en total
correlación con el estado de reflexión de su estómago; y si al mismo tiempo
es algo aventurero,en ese lapso puede acumular cosas que talvez irresen a
otras personas y cuyo relato indiscriminado costituiría algo así como estas
notas.

Así, la moneda fué por el aire,dió muchas volteretas;cayó una vez
"cara"y alguna otra "seca"(en cantos es una forma de equilibrio que el hombre
no adopta sino cuando está,en fuga,como la moneda,hacia la alcantarilla de u-
na calle cualquiera). El hombre,medida de todas las cosas,habla aquí por mi
boca y relata en mi lenguaje lo que mis ojos vieron; a lo mejor sobre diez "ca-
ras" posibles solo vi una "seca",o viceversa,es posible y no hay atenuantes;
mi boca narra lo que mis ojos le contaron. Nuestra vista nunca fué panorámica,
siempre fugaz y no siempre equitativamente informada,los juicios son demasiado
terminantes; de acuerdo, pero ésta es la interpretación que un teclado da al
conjunto de los impulsos que llevaron a apretar las teclas y esos fugaces impulsos han muerto. No hay sujeto sobre quien ejercer el peso de la ley. El
personaje que escribió estas notas murió al pisar de nuevo tierra Argentina,
el que las ordena y pule eso, "yo",no soy yo;por lo menos no soy el mismo yo
interior.Ese vagar sin por nuestra "Mayúscula América" me ha cambiado
más de lo que creí. En cualquier libro de técnica fotográfica se puede ver la
de un nocturno en el que brilla la luna llena y cuyo texto ex-
plicativo nos revela el secreto de esa nocturno a medio día,pero la naturale-
za del baño sensitivo conque está cubierto mi retina no es conocida por
apenas la intuyo,de modo que no se puede hacer correcciones sobre la pla-
para averiguar el momento real en que fué sacado. Si presento un nocturno
créanlo o revienten,poco importa;que si no conocen personalmente el paisa-
de fotografiado por mis notas,difícilmente conocerán otra verdad que les que
les cuento aquí. Ahora los dejo con migo mismo;el que fuí....

san martín
de los andes

The road snakes between the low foothills that sound the beginning of the great cordillera of the Andes, then descends steeply until it reaches an unattractive, miserable town, surrounded in sharp contrast by magnificent, densely wooded mountains. San Martín lies on the yellow-green slopes that melt into the blue depths of Lake Lacar, a narrow tongue of water 35 meters wide and 500 kilometers long. The day it was "discovered" as a tourist haven the town's climate and transport difficulties were solved and its subsistence secured.

Our first attack on the local clinic completely failed but we were told to try the same tactic at the National Park's' offices. The superintendent of the park allowed us to stay in one of the tool sheds. The nightwatchman arrived, a huge, fat man weighing 140 kilos with a face as hard as nails, but he treated us very amiably, granting us permission to cook in his hut. That first night passed perfectly. We slept in the shed, content and warm on straw — certainly necessary in those parts where the nights are particularly cold.

We bought some beef and set off to walk along the shores of the lake. In the shade of the immense trees, where the wilderness had arrested the advance of civilization, we made plans to build a laboratory in this place, when we finished our trip. We imagined great windows that would take in the whole lake, winter

blanketing the ground in white; the dinghy we would use to travel from one side to the other; catching fish from a little boat; everlasting excursions into the almost virgin forest.

Although often on our travels we longed to stay in the formidable places we visited, only the Amazon jungle called out to that sedentary part of ourselves as strongly as did this place.

I now know, by an almost fatalistic conformity with the facts, that my destiny is to travel, or perhaps it's better to say that traveling is our destiny, because Alberto is the same as me. Still, there are moments when I think with profound longing of those wonderful areas in our south. Perhaps one day, tired of circling the world, I'll return to Argentina and settle on the Andean lakes, if not indefinitely then at least for a pause while I shift from one understanding of the world to another.

At dusk we started back and it was dark before we arrived. We were pleasantly surprised to find that Don Pedro Olate, the nightwatchman, had prepared a wonderful barbecue to treat us. We bought wine to return the gesture and ate like lions, just for a change. We were discussing how tasty the meat was and how soon we wouldn't be eating as extravagantly as we had done in Argentina, when Don Pedro told us he'd been asked to organize a barbecue for the drivers of a motor race taking place on the local

track that coming Sunday. He wanted two helpers and offered us the job. "Mind that I can't pay you, but you can stock up on meat for later."

It seemed like a good idea and we accepted the jobs of first and second assistants to the "Granddaddy of the Southern Argentine Barbecue."

Both assistants waited for Sunday with a kind of religious enthusiasm. At six in the morning on the day, we started our first job — loading wood on to a truck and taking it to the barbecue site — and we didn't stop work until 11 a.m. when the distinctive signal was given and everyone threw themselves voraciously at the tasty ribs.

A very strange person was giving orders, someone whom I addressed with the utmost respect as "Señora" any time I said a word, until one of my fellow workers said: "Hey kid, che, don't push Don Pendón too far, he'll get angry."

"Who's Don Pendón?" I asked, with the kind of gesture some uncultured kid would give. The answer, that Don Pendón was the "señora," left me cold, but not for long.

As always at barbecues, there was far too much meat for everyone, so we were given carte blanche to pursue our vocation as camels. We executed, furthermore, a carefully calculated plan. I pretended to get drunker and drunker and, with every apparent attack of nausea, I staggered off to the stream, a bottle of red wine

La Poderosa II, another of Ernesto's Rocinantes. Córdoba, Argentina, 1951.

hidden inside my leather jacket.

After five attacks of this type we had same number of liters of wine stored beneath the fronds of a willow, keeping cool in the water. When everything was over and the moment came to pack up the truck and return to town, I kept up my part, working reluctantly and bickering constantly with Don Pendón. To finish my performance I lay down flat on my back in the grass, utterly unable to take another step. Alberto, acting like a true friend, apologized for my behavior to the boss and stayed behind to look after me as the truck left. When the noise of the engine faded in the distance we jumped up and raced off like colts to the wine that would guarantee us several days of kingly consumption.

Alberto made it first and threw himself under the willow: his face was straight out of a comic film. Not a single bottle remained. Either my drunken state hadn't fooled anyone, or someone had seen me sneak off with the wine. The fact was, we were as broke as ever, retracing in our minds the smiles that had greeted my drunken antics, trying to find some trace of the irony with which we could identify the thief. To no avail. Lugging the chunk of bread and cheese we'd received and a few kilos of meat for the night, we had to walk back to town. We were well-fed and well-watered, but with our tails between our legs, not so much for the wine but for the fools they'd made of us. Words cannot describe it!...

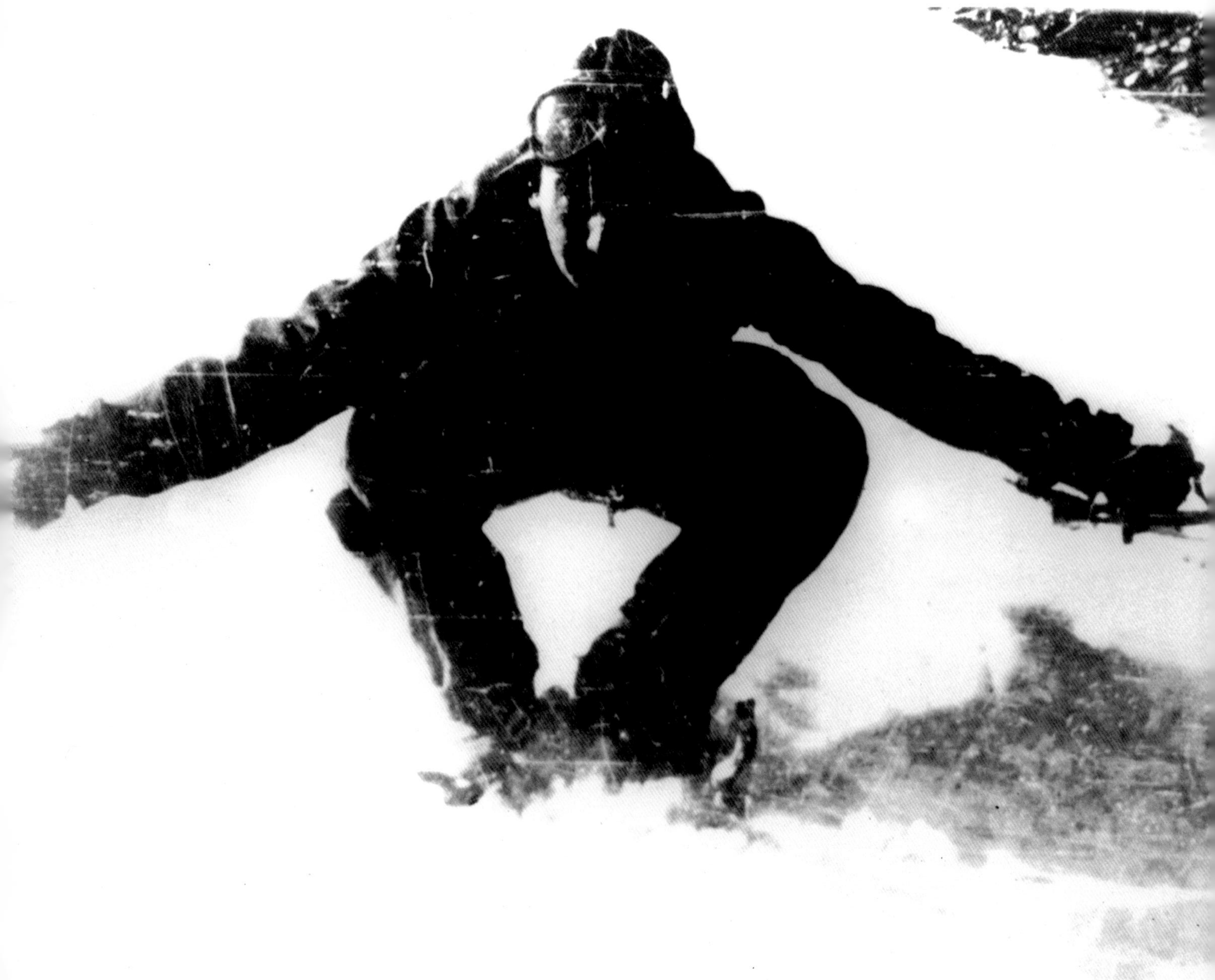

theseven lakesroad

We decided to go to Bariloche by the Seven Lakes road, named for the number of lakes the road skirts before reaching the town. We traveled the first few kilometers at La Poderosa's ever tranquil pace, without any serious mechanical upsets until, with nightfall chasing us down, we pulled the old broken headlight trick so we could sleep in a road laborer's hut, a handy ruse, because the cold that night was uncommonly harsh. It was so fiercely cold that a visitor soon appeared asking to borrow some blankets because he and his wife were camping by the edge of lake and were freezing. We went to share some *mate* with this stoical pair, who for some time had been living beside the lakes with only a tent and the contents of their backpacks. They put us to shame.

We set off again, passing greatly varying lakes, all surrounded by ancient forest, the scent of wilderness caressing our nostrils. But curiously, the sight of a lake and a forest and a single solitary house with well-tended garden soon begins to grate. Seeing the landscape at this superficial level only captures its boring uniformity, not allowing you to immerse yourself in the spirit of the place; for that you must stop at least several days.

We finally reached the northern end of Lake Nahuel Huapí and slept on its banks, full and content after the enormous barbecue we had eaten.

But when we hit the road again, we noticed a puncture in the back tire and from then began a tedious battle with the inner tube. Each time we patched up one side, the other side of the tube punctured, until we were all out of patches and were forced to spend the night where we were.

An Austrian caretaker who had raced motorbikes as a young man gave us a place to stay in an empty shed, caught between his desire to help fellow bikers in need and fear of his boss.

In his broken Spanish he told us that a puma was in the region. "And pumas are vicious, they're not afraid to attack people! They have huge blond manes..."

Attempting to close the door we found that it was like a stable door — only the lower half shut. I placed our revolver near my head in case the puma, whose shadow filled our thoughts, decided to pay an unannounced midnight visit. The day was just dawning when I awoke to the sound of claws scratching at the door. At my side, Alberto lay silent, full of dread. I had my hand tense on the cocked revolver. Two luminous eyes stared at me from the silhouetted trees. Like a cat, the eyes sprang forward and the black mass of the body materialized over the door.

It was pure instinct; the brakes of intelligence failed. My drive for self-preservation pulled the trigger.

For a long moment, the thunder beat against and around the walls, stopping only when a lighted torch in the doorway began desperately shouting at us. But by that time in our timid silence we knew, or could at least guess, the reason for the caretaker's stentorian shouts and his wife's hysterical sobs as she threw herself over the dead body of Bobby — her nasty, ill-tempered dog.

Alberto went to Angostura to get the tire fixed and I thought I'd have to spend the night in the open, being unable to ask for a bed in a house where we were considered murderers. Luckily our bike was near another road laborer's hut and he let me sleep in the kitchen with a friend of his. At midnight I woke to the noise of rain and was going to get up to cover the bike with a tarpaulin. But before doing so, I decided to take a few puffs from my asthma inhaler, irritated by the sheepskin I was using for a pillow. As I inhaled, my sleeping companion woke up, hearing the puff. He made a sudden movement, then immediately fell silent. I sensed his body go rigid under his blankets, clutching a knife, holding his breath. With the experience of the previous night still fresh, I decided to remain where I was, for fear of being knifed, in case mirages were contagious in those parts...

Left: Climbing the Argentine Andes, January 1952.

lagioconda's smile

We had come to a new phase in our adventure. We were used to calling idle attention to ourselves with our strange dress and the prosaic figure of La Poderosa II, whose asthmatic wheezing aroused pity in our hosts. To a certain extent we had been knights of the road; we belonged to that long-standing "wandering aristocracy" and had calling cards with our impeccable and impressive titles. No longer. Now we were just two hitchhikers with backpacks, and with all the grime of the road stuck to our overalls, shadows of our former aristocratic selves.

The truck driver had left us at the upper edge of the city, at its entrance, and with weary steps we dragged our packs down the streets, followed by the amused or indifferent glances of onlookers. In the distance the harbor radiated with the tempting glimmer of its boats, while the sea, black and inviting, cried out to us — its gray

smell dilating our nostrils. We bought bread — which seemed so expensive at the time though it became cheaper as we ventured further north — and kept walking downhill. Alberto wore his exhaustion obviously, and although I tried not to show it I was just as tired. So when we found a truck stop we assaulted the attendant with our tragic faces, relating in florid detail the hardships we had suffered on the long hard road from Santiago. He let us sleep on some wooden planks, in the company of some parasites whose name ends in *hominis*, but at least we had a roof over our heads.

We set about sleeping with determination. News of our arrival, however, reached the ears of a fellow countryman installed in a cheap restaurant next to the trailer park, and he wanted to meet us. To meet in Chile signifies a certain hospitality and neither of us was in a position to turn down this manna from heaven.

Our compatriot proved to be profoundly imbued with the spirit of the sisterland and consequently was fantastically drunk. It was a long time since I'd eaten fish, and the wine was so delicious, and our host so attentive... Anyway, we ate well and he invited us to his house the following day.

La Gioconda threw open its doors early and we brewed our *mate*, chatting with the owner who was very interested in our journey. After that, we went to explore the city. Valparaíso is very picturesque, built to the edge of the beach and overlooking a large bay. As it grew it clambered up the hills that sweep down to their deaths in the sea. The madhouse museum beauty of its strange corrugated iron architecture, arranged on a series of tiers linked by winding flights of stairs and funiculars, is heightened by the contrast of diversely colored houses blending with the leaden blue of the bay. As if patiently dissecting, we pry into dirty stairways and dark recesses, talking to the swarms of beggars; we plumb the city's depths, the miasma that draws us in. Our distended nostrils inhale the poverty with sadistic intensity...

We tried to contact the doctors from Petrohué, but being back at work with no time to spare, they never agreed to meet us formally. At least we knew more or less where they were. In the afternoon we went our separate ways: while Alberto followed up the doctors, I went to see an old woman with asthma, a customer at La Gioconda. The poor thing was in a pitiful state, breathing the acrid smell of concentrated sweat and dirty feet that filled her room, mixed with the dust from a couple of armchairs, the only luxury items in her house. On top of her asthma, she had a heart condition. It is at times like this, when a doctor is conscious of his complete powerlessness, that he longs for change: a change to prevent the injustice of a system in which only a month ago this poor woman was still earning her living as a waitress, wheezing and panting but facing life with dignity. In circumstances like this, individuals in poor families who can't pay their way become surrounded by an atmosphere of barely disguised acrimony; they stop being father, mother, sister or brother and become a purely negative factor in the struggle for life and, consequently, a source of bitterness for the healthy members of the community who resent their illness as if it were a personal insult to those who have to support them. It is there, in the final moments, for people whose farthest horizon has always been tomorrow, that one comprehends the profound tragedy circumscribing the life of the proletariat the world over. In those dying eyes there is a submissive appeal for forgiveness and also, often, a desperate plea for consolation which is lost to the void, just as their body will soon be lost in the magnitude of mystery surrounding us. How long this present order, based on an absurd idea of caste, will last is not within my means to answer, but it's time that those who govern spent less time publicizing their own virtues and more money, much more money, funding socially useful works.

There isn't much I can do for the sick woman. I simply advise her to improve her diet and prescribe a diuretic and some asthma pills. I have a few Dramamine tablets left and I give them to her. When I leave, I am followed by the fawning words of the old woman and the family's indifferent gaze...

this time, disaster

I can see him now, clearly, the drunk captain, like all his officers and the owner of the vessel alongside with his great big mustache, their crude gestures the results of bad wine. And the wild laughter as they recounted our odyssey. "Hey listen, they're tigers, they're on your boat now for sure, you'll find out when you're out to sea." The captain must have let slip to his friend and colleague this or some similar phrase. We didn't, of course, know any of this; an hour before sailing we were comfortably installed, totally buried in tons of perfumed melons, stuffing ourselves silly. We were talking about the sailors, who were the best, since with the complicity of one of them we had been able to get on board and hide ourselves away in such a very secure spot. And then we heard an irate voice, and a seemingly enormous mustache emerged from who knows where and plunged us into an appalling confusion. A long line of melon skins, perfectly peeled, was floating away Indian file on the tranquil sea. The rest was ignominious. The sailor told us afterwards, "I'd have got him off the scent, boys, but he saw the melons and it seems he went into a "batten down the hatches, don't let anyone escape" routine. And well," (he was fairly embarrassed) "you shouldn't have eaten so many melons!"

One of our traveling companions from the *San Antonio* summed up his brilliant life philosophy with one fine phrase: "Stop assing about you assholes. Why don't you get off your asses and go back to your asshole

country." So that's more or less what we did; we picked up our bags and set off for Chuquicamata, the famous copper mine.

But not straight away. There was a break of one day while we waited for permission from the mine's authorities to visit and meanwhile we received an appropriate send-off from the enthusiastic Bacchanalian sailors.

Lying beneath the meager shade of two lampposts on the arid road leading to the mines, we spent a good part of the day yelling things at each other now and again from one post to another, until on the horizon appeared the asthmatic outline of the little truck which took us halfway, to a town called Baquedano.

There we made friends with a married couple, Chilean workers who were communists. By the light of the single candle illuminating us, drinking *mate* and eating a piece of bread and cheese, the man's shrunken figure carried a mysterious, tragic air. In his simple and expressive language he recounted his three months in prison, and told us about his starving wife who stood by him with exemplary loyalty, his children — left in the care of a kindly neighbor, his fruitless pilgrimage in search of work and his *compañeros*, mysteriously disappeared and said to be somewhere at the bottom of the sea.

The couple, numb with cold, huddling against each other in the desert night, were a living representation of the proletariat in any part of the world. They had not one single miserable

blanket to cover themselves with, so we gave them one of ours and Alberto and I wrapped the other around us as best we could. It was one of the coldest times in my life, but also one which made me feel a little more brotherly toward this strange, for me anyway, human species.

At eight the next morning we found a truck to take us to the town of Chuquicamata. We separated from the couple who were heading for the sulphur mines in the mountains, where the climate is so bad and the living conditions so hard that you don't need a work permit and nobody asks you what your politics are. The only thing that matters is the enthusiasm with which the worker sets to ruining his health in search of a few meager crumbs that barely provide his subsistence.

Although the blurred silhouette of the couple was nearly lost in the distance separating us, we could still see the man's singularly determined face and we remembered his straightforward invitation: "Come, comrades, let's eat together. I, too, am a tramp," which showed his underlying disdain for the parasitic nature he saw in our aimless traveling.

It's a great pity that they repress people like this. Apart from whether collectivism, the "communist vermin," is a danger to decent life, the communism gnawing at his entrails was no more than a natural longing for something better, a protest against persistent hunger transformed into a love for this strange doctrine, whose essence he could never grasp but whose translation, "bread for the poor," was something he understood and, more importantly, that filled him with hope.

There, the bosses, the blond, efficient and arrogant managers, told us in primitive Spanish: "This isn't a tourist town. I'll find a guide to give you a half-hour tour around the mine's installations and then do us a favor and leave us alone, we have a lot of work to do." A strike was imminent. Yet the guide, faithful dog of the Yankee bosses, told us: "Imbecilic gringos, losing thousands of *pesos* every day in a strike so as not to give a poor worker a few more *centavos*. When my General Ibáñez comes to power that'll all be over."

And a foreman-poet: "These are the famous grades that enable every inch of copper to be mined. Many people like you ask me technical questions but it is rare they ask how many lives it has cost. I can't answer you, doctors, but thank you for asking."

Cold efficiency and impotent resentment go hand in hand in the big mine, linked in spite of the hatred by the common necessity to live, on the one hand, and to speculate on the other... we will see whether one day, some miner will take up his pick in pleasure and go and poison his lungs with a conscious joy. They say that's what it's like over there, where the red blaze that now lights up the world comes from. So they say. I don't know.

chile, a vision from afar

When I made these travel notes, hot and fresh with enthusiasm, I wrote some things that were perhaps a little flashy and somewhat removed from the intended spirit of scientific inquiry. And it's probably not appropriate now, more than a year after writing them, to give my current opinions about Chile; I'd prefer to review what I wrote then.

Beginning with our expertise, medicine: the panorama of health care in Chile leaves a lot to be desired (although I realized later it was by far superior to that in other countries I got to know). Free, public hospitals are extremely rare and even in those posters announcing the following appear: "Why do you complain about your treatment if you are not contributing to the maintenance of this hospital?" Generally speaking, medical attention in the north is free, but hospital accommodation has to be paid for, and prices range from petty

sums to virtual monuments to legalized theft. Sick or injured workers at the Chuquicamata mine receive medical attention and hospital treatment for five Chilean *escudos* a day, but someone not working at the mine would pay between 300 and 500 *escudos* a day. Hospitals have no money and they lack medicine and adequate facilities. We have seen filthy operating rooms with pitiful lighting, and not just in small towns but even in Valparaíso. There aren't enough surgical instruments. The bathrooms are dirty. Awareness of hygiene is poor. It's a Chilean custom (afterwards I saw it across practically all of South America) not to throw used toilet paper in the toilet but on to the floor or in the boxes provided.

The standard of living in Chile is lower than in Argentina. On top of the very low wages paid in the south, unemployment is high and the authorities afford workers very

little protection (although it's better than is provided in the north of the continent). Veritable waves of Chileans are driven by all this into emigrating to Argentina, in search of the legendary city of gold which cunning political propaganda has offered those who live to the west of the Andes. In the north, workers in the copper, nitrate, gold and sulphur mines are better paid, but life is much more expensive, and they lack in general many essential consumer items and the mountain climate is cruel. It brings to mind the meaningful shrug with which a manager at Chuquicamata answered my questions regarding compensation paid to the families of the 10,000 or more workers interred in the local cemetery.

The political scene is confusing (this was written before the elections in which Ibáñez triumphed). There are four presidential candidates, of whom

Carlos Ibáñez del Campo seems most likely to win. A retired soldier with dictatorial tendencies and political ambitions similar to those of Perón, he inspires his people with all the enthusiasm of a caudillo. His base of power is the Popular Socialist Party, behind which various minor factions are united. Second in line, as far as I can see, is Pedro Enrique Alfonso, the official government candidate, who is politically ambiguous; he seems to be friendly with the Americans and courts almost all the other parties. The champion of the right is the tycoon Arturo Matte Larraín, the son-in-law of the late President Alessandri who counts the support of all the reactionary sectors of the population. Last on the list is the Popular Front candidate Salvador Allende, who is supported by the communists even though they have seen their voting power reduced by 40,000, the number of people denied the right to vote because of their affiliation to the Communist Party.

It's likely that Ibáñez will observe a politics of Latin Americanism, manipulating hatred of the United States to gain popularity; nationalizing the copper mines and others (although the fact that the United States owns huge Peruvian mineral deposits and is practically ready to begin exploiting them, doesn't greatly increase my confidence that nationalization of these Chilean mines will be feasible, at least in the short term); continue nationalizing the railroads and substantially enlarge Argentine-Chilean trade.

Chile as a country offers economic promise to any person disposed to work for it, so long as they don't belong to the proletariat: I mean, anyone who has a certain dose of education and technical knowledge. The land has the capacity to sustain enough livestock (especially sheep) and cereals to provide for its population. There are the necessary mineral resources to transform it into a powerful industrial country: iron, copper, coal, tin, gold, silver, manganese and nitrates. The biggest effort Chile should make is to shake its uncomfortable Yankee friend from its back, a task that for the moment at least is Herculean, given the quantity of dollars the United States has invested here and the ease with which it flexes its economic muscle whenever its interests seem threatened.

thenavel
oftheworld

The word that most perfectly describes the city of Cuzco is evocative. Intangible dust of another era settles on its streets, rising like the disturbed sediment of a muddy lake when you touch its bottom. But there are two or three Cuzcos, or it's better to say, two or three ways the city can be summoned. When Mama Oello dropped her golden wedge into the soil and it sank effortlessly, the first Incas knew this was the place selected by Viracocha to be the permanent home for his chosen ones, who had left behind their nomadic lives to come as conquistadors to their promised land. With nostrils flaring zealously for new horizons, they watched as their formidable empire grew, always looking beyond the feeble barrier of the surrounding mountains. And the converted nomads set to expanding Tahuantinsuyo, fortifying as they did so the center of their conquered territory — the navel of the world —

Cuzco. And here grew, as a necessary defense for the empire, the imposing Sacsahuamán, dominating the city from its heights and protecting the palaces and temples from the wrath of the enemies of the empire. The vision of this Cuzco emerges mournfully from the fortress destroyed by the stupidity of illiterate Spanish conquistadors, from the violated ruins of the temples, from the sacked palaces, from the faces of a brutalized race. This is the Cuzco inviting you to become a warrior and to defend, club in hand, the freedom and the life of the Inca.

High above the city another Cuzco can be seen, displacing the destroyed fortress: a Cuzco with colored-tile roofs, its gentle uniformity interrupted by the cupola of a baroque church; and as the city falls away it shows us only its narrow streets and its native inhabitants dressed in typical costume, all the

local colors. This Cuzco invites you to be a hesitant tourist, to pass over things superficially and to relax into the beauty beneath a leaden winter sky.

And there is yet another Cuzco, a vibrant city whose monuments bear witness to the formidable courage of the warriors who conquered the region in the name of Spain, the Cuzco to be found in museums and libraries, in the church facades and in the clear, sharp features of the white chiefs who even today feel pride in the conquest. This is the Cuzco asking you to pull on your armor and, mounted on the ample back of a powerful horse, cleave a path through the defenseless flesh of a naked Indian flock whose human wall collapses and disappears beneath the four hooves of the galloping beast.

Each one of these Cuzcos can be admired separately, and to each one we dedicated a part of our stay.

Right: Toward the navel of the world. Cuzco, Peru, 1952.

lord of the earthquakes

From the cathedral, the peals of the Maria Angola rang out for the first time since the earthquake. Legend has it that this famous bell, among the largest in the world, contains 27 kilograms of gold. It was supposedly donated by a lady called María Angulo, but the name of the bell itself was changed due to a slight problem with rhyming slang.*

The cost of restoring the cathedral bell towers, destroyed by the earthquake of 1950, had been met by General Franco's government, and as a gesture of gratitude the band was ordered to play the Spanish national anthem. As the first chords sounded, the bishop's red headdress locked itself into position as he moved his arms about like a puppet. "Stop, stop, there's been a mistake," he whispered, while the indignant voice of a Spaniard could be heard, "Two years' work, and they play this!" I couldn't

say whether with good intentions or otherwise, the band had struck up the Spanish Republican anthem.

In the afternoon he leaves his stately home in the cathedral, Our Lord of the Earthquakes, who is no more than a dark brown image of Christ. He is paraded throughout the city and his pilgrimage stops at all the main churches. As he passes, a crowd of layabouts competes with each other to throw handfuls of the little flowers that grow abundantly on the slopes of the nearby mountains, named *nucchu* by the natives. The violent red of the flowers, the intense bronze of the Lord of the Earthquakes and the silver altar they carry him on lend the impression that the procession is a pagan festival, a feeling that is intensified by the many-colored clothes of the Indians, who wear for the occasion their best traditional costumes in expression of a culture

or way of life which still holds on to living values. In contrast, a cluster of Indians in European clothes march at the head of the procession, carrying banners. Their tired, affected faces resemble an image of those Quechuas who refused to heed Manco II's call, pledging themselves to Pizarro and in the degradation of their defeat smothering the pride of an independent race.

Standing over the small frames of the Indians gathered to see the procession pass, the blond head of a North American can occasionally be glimpsed, who, with his camera and sports shirt, seems to be (and, in fact, actually is) a correspondent from another world lost amid the isolation of the Inca Empire.

* Because it rhymed with *culo* (ass in Spanish).

Left: In the Land of the Incas, on the road from Taratá to Puno, Peru, 1952.

saintguevara'sday

On Saturday, June 14, 1952, I, just a lad, turned 24, on the cusp of that transcendental quarter century, silver wedding of a life, which, all things considered, has not treated me so badly. Early in the morning I went to the river, to try my luck again with the fish, but that sport is like gambling: one starts out winning and ends up losing. In the afternoon we played football and I occupied my usual place in goal, with better results than on earlier occasions. In the evening, after passing by Dr. Bresciani's house for a delightful, huge meal, they threw a party for us in the dining room of the [leper] colony, with a lot of the Peruvian national drink, *pisco*. Alberto is quite experienced regarding its effects on the central nervous system. With everyone slightly drunk and in high spirits, the colony's

director toasted us warmly, and I, "piscoed," replied with something elaborate, like the following:

Well, it's my duty to respond to the toast offered by Dr. Bresciani with something more than a conventional gesture. In our presently precarious state as travelers, we only have recourse to words and I would now like to use them to express my thanks, and those of my traveling compañero, to all of the staff the colony who, almost without knowing us, have given us this beautiful demonstration of their affection, celebrating my birthday as if it were an intimate celebration for one of your own. But there is something more. Within a few days we will be leaving Peruvian territory, so these words have the secondary intention of being a farewell, and I would like to stress our gratitude to all the people of this country, who have unfailingly shown us their warmest hospitality since we entered Peru via Tacna.

I would also like to say something else, unrelated to the theme of this toast. Although our insignificance means we can't be spokespeople for such a noble cause, we believe, and after this journey more firmly than ever, that the division of America into unstable and illusory nations is completely fictional. We constitute a single mestizo race, which from Mexico to the Magellan Straits bears notable ethnographical similarities. And so, in an attempt to rid myself of the weight of small-minded provincialism, I propose a toast to Peru and to a United Latin America.

My oratory offering was received with great applause. The party, consisting in these parts of drinking as much alcohol as possible, continued until three in the morning, when we finally called it a day...

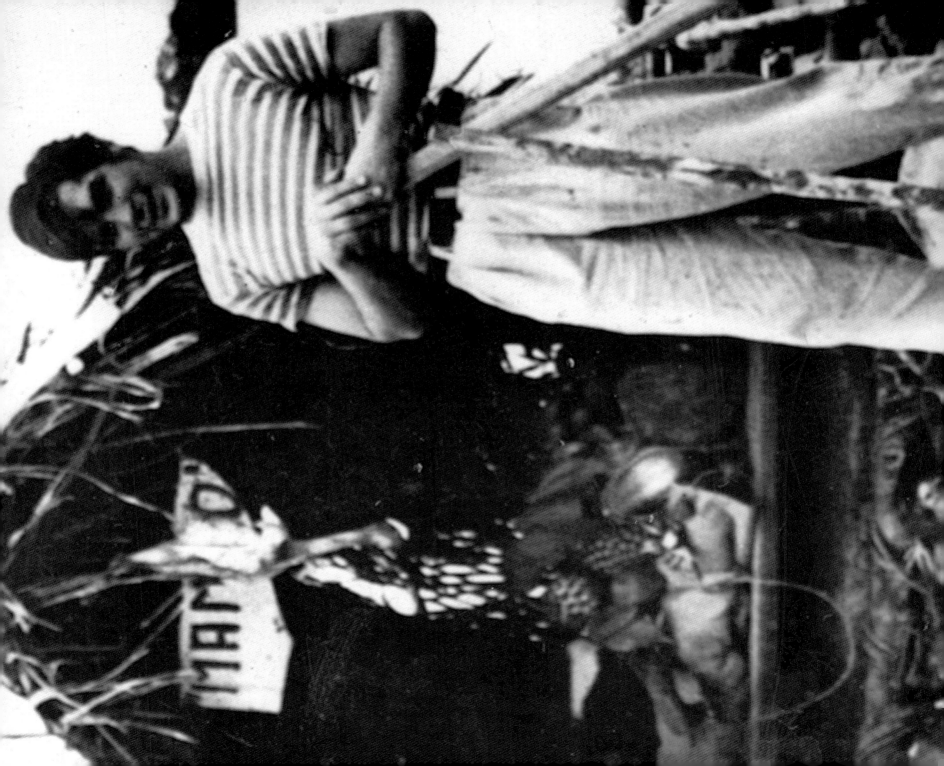

The worst of my asthma attack has now passed and I feel almost well, though sometimes I resort to my new acquisition, a French inhaler. I feel Alberto's absence so sharply. It seems like my flanks are unguarded from some hypothetical attack. At every other moment I'm turning around to share an observation with him only to realize he's not there.

It's true, there's not really much to complain about: thoroughly looked after, good food and a lot of it, and the anticipation of returning home to start studying again and to obtain the degree which will enable me to practise. Yet the idea of splitting up definitively doesn't make me completely happy; the many months we've been side by side, through good and bad, accustomed to dreaming similar dreams in similar situations, have brought us so much closer together. With these ideas constantly turning over in my mind, I find myself

drifting away from the center of Caracas. The homes in the suburbs are spaced much further apart. Caracas extends along the length of a narrow valley, enclosing and restraining it on its edges, so that on a short walk you'll be climbing the surrounding hills, and there, with the progressive city laid out before your feet, you'll begin to see a new aspect of its multifaceted makeup. The blacks, those magnificent examples of the African race who have maintained their racial purity thanks to their lack of an affinity with bathing, have seen their territory invaded by a new kind of slave: the Portuguese. And the two ancient races have now begun a hard life together, fraught with bickering and squabbles. Discrimination and poverty unite them in the daily fight for survival but their different ways of approaching life separate them completely: the black is indolent and a dreamer; spending his meager wage

on frivolity or drink; the European has a tradition of work and saving, which has pursued him as far as this corner of the Americas and drives him to advance himself, even independently of his own individual aspirations.

At this elevation the concrete houses have totally disappeared and only adobe huts reign. I peer into one of them. It is a room half separated by a partition, with a fireplace and table and a heap of straw on the ground, apparently serving as beds. Various bony cats and a mangy dog play with three completely naked black children. Rising from the fire, acrid smoke fills the room. The black mother, frizzy hair and sagging breasts, is cooking, assisted by a girl of about 15, who is dressed. At the door of the hut we get into a conversation and after a while I ask if they will pose for a photo, which they categorically refuse to do unless I give it to them straight away. In vain I try to explain that I have to develop it first, but no, they want it then and there, or no ball game. Eventually I promise to hand it over straight away, but now they are suspicious and don't want to cooperate. One of the kids escapes to play with his friends while I continue chatting with the family. In the end, I stand guard at the door, camera in hand, pretending to snap anyone who pokes out their head. We play around like this for a while until I see the little kid returning carefree on a new bicycle; I focus and press the button but the effect is disastrous. To elude the photo, the kid swerves and falls to the ground, bursting into tears. Immediately they all lose their fear of the camera and rush out to hurl abuse at me. I withdraw somewhat apprehensively because they are excellent stone throwers, followed by the insults of the group — including the height of contempt: "Portuguese."

Littered along the edges of the road are containers for transporting cars, used by the Portuguese as dwellings. In one of these, where a black family lives, I can just glimpse a brand new refrigerator, and from many of them radios blare music which their owners play at maximum volume. New cars are parked outside the most miserable "homes." All kinds of aircraft pass overhead, sowing the air with noise and silver reflections and there, at my feet, lies Caracas, city of the eternal spring. Its center is threatened by the invasion of red tiled roofs that converge with the flat roofs of modern buildings. But something else will allow the yellowy color of its colonial buildings to live on, even after they have disappeared from the city maps: the spirit of Caracas, impervious to the lifestyle of the North and stubbornly rooted in the retrograde semi-pastoral conditions of its colonial past.

a note in the margin

The stars drew light across the night sky in that little mountain village, and the silence and the cold made the darkness vanish. It was — I don't know how to explain it — as if everything solid melted away into the ether, eliminating all individuality and absorbing us, rigid, into the immense darkness. Not a single cloud to lend perspective to the space blocked any portion of the starry sky. Less than a few meters away the dim light of a lamp lost its power to fade the darkness.

The man's face was indistinct in the shadows; I could only see what seemed like the spark of his eyes and the gleam of his four front teeth. I still can't say whether it was the atmosphere or the personality of that individual that prepared me for the revelation, but I know that many times and from many different people I had heard those same arguments and that they had never made an impression on me. Our interlocutor was, in fact, a very interesting character. From a country in Europe, he escaped the knife of dogmatism as a young man, he knew the taste of fear (one of the few experiences that makes one value life), and afterwards he had wandered from country to country, gathering thousands of adventures, until he and his bones finally ended up in this isolated region, patiently waiting for the moment of great reckoning to arrive.

After exchanging a few meaningless words and platitudes, each of us marking territory, the discussion began to falter and we were about to go our separate ways, when he let out his idiosyncratic, childlike laugh, highlighting the asymmetry of his four front incisors: "The future belongs to the people, and gradually, or in one strike, they will take power, here and in every country.

"The terrible thing is, the people need to be educated, and this they cannot do before taking power, only after. They can only learn at the cost of their own mistakes, which will be very serious and will cost many innocent lives. Or perhaps not, maybe those lives will not have been innocent because they will have committed the huge sin against nature; meaning, a lack of ability to adapt. All of them, those unable to adapt — you and I, for example — will die cursing the power they helped, through great sacrifice, to create. Revolution is impersonal; it will take their lives, even utilizing their memory as an example or as an instrument for domesticating the youth who follow them. My sin is greater because I, more astute and with greater experience, call it what you like, will die knowing that my sacrifice stems only from an inflexibility symbolizing our rotten civilization, which is crumbling. I also know —

Right: From Ernesto Guevara's original manuscript of *The Motorcycle Diaries*.

ACOTACION AL MARGEN

No había nada de escribir en la noche. Las estrellas veteaban de luz el cielo de aquel pueblo serrano y el silencio y el frío ir realizaban la oscuridad. Era-no se bien como explicarlo-como si nro se volatilizara en el espacio etéreo que nos ro- deaba, que nos quitaba la individualidad y nos sumía, yertos, en la in- mensidad, sin límites ¿...escogida? No había una nube que, bloque- ando una poción de cielo estrellado, diera perspectiva al espacio. A- penas a unos metros, la mortecina luz de un farol desteñía las tinie- blas circundantes.

La cara del hombre se perdía en la sombra, solo emergían unos como destellos de sus ojos y la blancura de los cuatro dientes delanteros. Todavía no se si fué el ambiente o la personalidad del individuo el que preparó para recibir la revelación, pero se que los argumentos empleados los había oído muchas veces esgrimidos por personas diferentes y nunca me habían impresionado. En realidad, era una personalidad interesante nuestro interlocutor: desde joven

huído de un país de Europa para escapar al cuchillo dogmatizante, cono- cía el sabor del miedo(unas de las pocas experiencias que hacen valo- cía el sabor del miedo(unas de las pocas experiencias que hacen valo- rar la vida) despues, rodando de país en país había dado con sus huesos en esa apartada región y allí esperaba pacientemente el momento del gran acontecimiento.

Despues de las frases triviales y los lugares comunes con que cada uno planteó su posición, cuando ya languidecía la discu- sión y estábamos por separarnos, dejo caer, con la misma risa de chico pícaro que siempre lo acompañaba, acentuado la disparidad de sus cua- tro incisivos delanteros: "El porvenir es del pueblo y poco a poco o de golpe conquistar el poder aquí y en toda la tierra. Lo malo es que el pueblo que civilizarse y eso no se puede hacer antes si no despues de tomar el poder. Se civilizará sólo aprendiendo a cos- ta de sus propios errores, errores que serán muy graves, que costarán

and this won't alter the course of history or your personal view of me — that you will die with a clenched fist and a tense jaw, the epitome of hatred and struggle, because you are not a symbol (some inanimate example) but a genuine member of the society to be destroyed; the spirit of the beehive speaks through your mouth and motivates your actions. You are as useful as I am, but you are not aware of how useful your contribution is to the society that sacrifices you."

I saw his teeth and the cheeky grin with which he foretold history, I felt his handshake and, like a distant murmur, his formal goodbye. The night, folding in at contact with his words, overtook me again, enveloping me within it. But despite his words, I now knew... I knew that when the great guiding spirit cleaves humanity into two antagonistic halves, I would be with the people.

I know this, I see it printed in the night sky that I, eclectic dissembler of doctrine and psychoanalyst of dogma, howling like one possessed, will assault the barricades or the trenches, will take my bloodstained weapon and, consumed with fury, slaughter any enemy who falls into my hands. And I see, as if a great exhaustion smothers this fresh exaltation, I see myself, immolated in the genuine revolution, the great equalizer of individual will, proclaiming the ultimate *mea culpa*. I feel my nostrils dilate, savoring the acrid smell of gunpowder and blood, of the enemy's death; I steel my body, ready to do battle, and prepare myself to be a sacred space within which the bestial howl of the triumphant proletariat can resound with new energy and new hope.

Ernesto (center with cap), with Alberto Granado (front left),
La Poderosa II and friends, 1951.

Otra vez (Once Again) is the second Latin American travel diary written by the young Ernesto Guevara. The original document is held in his personal archives.

Ernesto began to write this diary as he left Buenos Aires on July 7, 1953, and continued until the birth of his daughter Hildita in Mexico on February 15, 1956. On that date, with great power, appear the premonitory words: "This year could be important for my future…"

Our book continues its explorations of Che's words and images with the following text: Ernesto Guevara's first encounter with La Paz, a city which came to form part of the last chapter of his life, that of the guerrilla struggle in Bolivia. In this prologue of sorts Che describes, with sobriety and emotion, "the formidable beauty of Illimani… perpetually illuminated by the halo of snow which nature has lent it for eternity." Che offers us three ways of looking at the world of Palenque, through an article he wrote,

a poem and some photographs he took of the pre-Columbian ruins. Piercing, informative and ironic, Che's letters and notes from an unfinished diary narrate his Central American and Mexican experiences, casting light on the future course of his thought and action.

—VC

THE JOURNEYS: **secondlookat latinamerica**

la paz, ingenuous, candid…

At four in the afternoon, the train approaches the gorge in which La Paz nestles. A small and very beautiful city spreads out over the valley's uneven terrain, with the eternally snowcapped figure of Illimani guarding over it. The final few kilometers take over an hour to complete. The train seems fixed on a tangent to avoid the city but then it turns and continues the descent.

It is a Saturday afternoon and very difficult for us to find the people we have been sent to see, so we devote our time to dressing and to ridding ourselves of the journey's grime.

We begin Sunday by going to see the people we have been introduced to, and by contacting the Argentine residents.

La Paz is the Shanghai of the Americas. Many adventurers, a wonderful range of all nationalities, have come here to stagnate or thrive in this polychromatic, racially mixed city that drives the country toward its destiny.

The so-called fine folk, the cultured people, have been surprised by events and curse the recognition now being paid to the Indian and the mestizo, but I vaguely divined in all of them a spark of nationalist enthusiasm with regard to some of the government's actions.

Nobody denies that the situation represented by the power of the three tin mine giants had to come to an end, and the young people believe that this has been a step forward in the struggle for greater equality between people and wealth.

On the night of July 15, there was a long and boring torchlight procession — a kind of demonstration — though of interest was the way in which it expressed support by firing shots from Mausers, or *Piri-pipi*, the terrible repeating guns.

The next day there was a never-ending parade of workers' guilds, schools and unions, with assiduous firings of the Mausers. Every few steps, one of the leaders of the companies into which the procession was divided would shout, "Comrades of such-and-such-a-guild, long live Bolivia! Glory be to the early

martyrs of our independence, Glory be to Pedro Domingo Murillo, Glory be to Guzmán, Glory be to Villarroel!" This recitative was delivered wearily, and accordingly a chorus of monotonous voices responded. It was a picturesque demonstration, but not particularly vigorous. Their weary way of walking and general lack of enthusiasm drained it of any vitality, while, according to those in the know, the energetic faces of the miners were missing.

On the morning of another day, we took a truck to Las Yungas. Initially, we climbed to 4,600 meters to a place called La Cumbre, and then moved slowly down a ridge road flanked

almost the whole way by a deep precipice. We spent two magnificent days in Las Yungas, but among our supplies we needed two women to provide that erotic nuance missing in all the green surrounding us everywhere we looked. On the green mountain slopes, plunging several hundred meters to the river below and guarded by an overcast sky, were scatterings of coconut stands in typical terraces; banana trees that, from the distance, looked like green propellers rising from the jungle; orange and other citrus trees; coffee trees rosy red with their beans and other fruit and tropical trees, all this

offset by the spindly form of a papaya tree, its shape somehow reminiscent of a static llama...

La Paz, ingenuous, candid as a young girl from the provinces, proudly shows off her marvelous public buildings. We check out the new constructions, the diminutive university overlooking the entire city from its courtyards, the municipal library, etc.

The formidable beauty of Illimani radiates a soft light, perpetually illuminated by the halo of snow which nature has lent it for eternity. It is when twilight falls that the mountain acquires the maximum force of its solemnity and power.

macchu-picchu, enigma in stone of the americas

Crowning a hill of steep and rugged slopes, 2,800 meters above sea level and 400 above the fast-flowing River Urubamba that bathes three sides of this high land, is the ancient city in stone that, by extension, has been given the name of the place that is its bastion: Macchu-Picchu.

Is this its original name? No. In Quechua, Macchu-Picchu means Old Mountain, as opposed to Huaina-Picchu, the rocky needle rising just a few meters from the settlement, which means Young Mountain. They are simply physical descriptions of the topographical features of the place. What would its real name be then? Let us diverge for a moment and travel back to the past.

The 16th century of our age was a tragic time for the indigenous peoples of the Americas. The bearded invader flooded the continent and the great indigenous empires were reduced to rubble. In the center of South America, the internecine struggle for power between the two candidates to inherit the crown of the deceased Huaina-Capac, Atahualpa and Huascar, made the business of destroying the greatest empire of the continent even easier.

In order to contain the human mass approaching perilously close to Cuzco, one of Huascar's nephews, the youthful Manco II, was placed on the throne by Spain. This maneuver had an unexpected sequel: although the indigenous people now had a visible head, bestowed with all the formalities of Inca law still possible under the Spanish yoke, the monarch was not as easy to control as the Spaniards wished. He disappeared one night with his leading chiefs, bearing with him the great disc of gold, symbol of the sun. From that day onward, there was no peace in the old capital of the empire.

There was no security, moving from one place to another was not safe. Armed bands used the ancient, impressive and now-destroyed Sacsahuamán as their base, the fortress guarding Cuzco. They roamed the territory and even moved in close to the city.

It was 1536.

This large-scale revolt failed, the siege of Cuzco had to be abandoned, and another major battle in Ollantaitambo, the walled city on the banks of the River Urubamba, was lost by the troops of the indigenous monarch. The threat of the guerrilla

war, which had been a considerable thorn in the side of Spanish might, was definitively reduced. One day, in a drunken outburst, one of the conquistador soldiers, a deserter who had been taken in by the indigenous court along with six of his companions, killed the Inca sovereign. He and his unfortunate compatriots were put to a horrible death by the indigenous subjects, who displayed their severed heads on their spears as both punishment and challenge. The sovereign's three sons, Sairy Tupac, Tito Cusi and Túpac Amaru, reigned consecutively and died while in power. With the third, however, something more than a monarch passed into death: it was the final demise of the Inca empire.

The forceful and inflexible viceroy, Francisco Toledo, took this last sovereign as his prisoner and had him executed in Cuzco's parade ground in 1572. The Inca king, whose life — secluded in the temple of the sun virgins, with a brief parenthesis as sovereign — ended so tragically, addressed his people in his final hour. His forceful speech roused them from their former torpor and meant that his name would be taken up again

Left: With Eduardo García (right), with whom Che traveled from Ecuador to Guatemala.

by the precursor of Latin American independence: José Gabriel Condorcanqui, Túpac Amaru II.

The danger to the representatives of the Spanish crown had been extinguished and nobody thought to seek out the old operational base of the Incas, the well-concealed city of Vilcapampa, whose last sovereign had left before being taken prisoner. Thus began a period of three centuries in which total silence reigned with respect to the city. When an Italian man of science, Antonio Raimondi, devoted 19 years of his life to traveling all over the country in the second half of the 19th century, Peru was a land still largely free of European traces. Though it is true Raimondi was not a professional archaeologist, his profound erudition and scientific skills gave an enormous impetus to the study of the country's Inca past. Generations of Peruvian students now turned their eyes to the heart of a country they did not know, guided by the monumental work *El Perú*, while scientists from all over the world once again recovered their enthusiasm for investigating the history of a great earlier race.

At the beginning of the 20th century, a U.S. historian, professor Bingham, who had come to Peru to study the routes taken *in situ* by [Simón] Bolívar, was captivated by the extraordinary beauty of the regions he visited and tempted by the provocative questions raised by Inca culture. Professor Bingham, satisfying both the historian and the adventurer within him, set out in search of the lost city, the operational base of the insurgent monarchs.

Bingham knew, from the chronicles of Father Calancha and others, that the Incas had a political and military capital they named Vitcos, and a more distant sanctuary called Vilcapampa, the city where no white person had ever set foot. Armed with this information, he set out on his search.

Anyone with even a superficial knowledge of the region will not be unaware of the magnitude of the task he had set himself. In mountainous terrain, covered with dense, subtropical forest, crisscrossed by rivers that were more like highly dangerous torrents, not knowing the psychology or even the language of its inhabitants, Bingham set off with three powerful weapons:

an indomitable zest for adventure, keen intuition and a healthy handful of dollars.

Patiently, paying a high price for each secret or piece of information he could extract, he penetrated the heartland of the extinct civilization. One day in 1911, after years of arduous labor, routinely following an Indian who was selling an unusual set of stones, Bingham, unaccompanied by any other white man, found himself marveling alone at the impressive ruins that, surrounded and almost submerged in undergrowth, were there to welcome him.

There is a sad side to this story. The undergrowth was cleared from the ruins, which were then studied and perfectly described... and totally stripped of whatever objects that turned up. Researchers triumphantly bore off to their country more than 200 crates of archaeological treasures that were both invaluable and, let us be clear about this, worth a great deal of money. Bingham is, objectively speaking, not specifically guilty of this and neither are the citizens of the United States guilty in general. Yet neither is a government without the economic resources to mount an expedition on a scale comparable to that of the discovery of Macchu-Picchu. Is no one guilty then? Let us just accept the fact that the answer to the question of where one might study or admire the treasures of the indigenous city is obvious: in the museums of the United States.

Macchu-Picchu was not just any old discovery for Bingham. It meant triumph, the crowning of an overgrown child's limpid dreams — like the dreams of almost all amateurs in this area of science. A long itinerary of triumph and failure culminated there, and the city of gray stone gathered before it all his fantasies and his watchfulness, thrusting him into comparison and conjecture that was at times far removed from careful and scientific description. The years of exploration and those that followed his success made an erudite archaeologist of the former traveler-historian; many of his assertions, backed by the formidable experience acquired in his travels, were taken as gospel truth in scientific circles.

In Bingham's view, Macchu-Picchu was the ancient abode of the Quechua people and the center from which they expanded before founding Cuzco. He delved into Inca mythology and identified three windows of a ruined temple as those from which the Ayllus brothers, characters in Inca mythology, had emerged. He found conclusive similarities between a circular tower in the newly revealed city and the Cuzco sun temple. He identified skeletons that had been found in the ruins, almost all of them female, as being those of the sun virgins. Finally, after carefully analyzing all the possibilities, he came to the following conclusion: the city he had discovered had been named Vilcapampa more than three centuries earlier. This, he said, had been the sanctuary of the rebel monarchs, and had previously served as a refuge for the vanquished followers of the Inca leader Pachacuti (whose body lay in the city) from the time of their defeat by Chincha troops until the resurgence of the empire. But the reason this city had in both cases been the refuge of vanquished warriors was because this was Tampu-Toco, sacred place and initial nucleus, located here and not at Pacaru Tampu, near Cuzco, as Indian notables told the historian Sarmiento de Gamboa, who interrogated them on the orders of Viceroy Toledo.

Modern researchers have disagreed on many points with the archaeologist from North America, but they have nothing to say about the definitive meaning of Macchu-Picchu.

After several hours on the train, an asthmatic thing, almost a toy, that runs first along a small river to continue later along the banks of the River Urubamba, passing the stately ruins of Ollantaitambo, it eventually comes to the bridge crossing the river. A winding track of some eight kilometers climbs 400 meters above the torrent, bringing us to the hotel in the ruins, which is run by a Señor Soto. He is a man of extraordinary knowledge in Inca matters, and a good singer, who contributes, in the delicious tropical evenings, to heightening the suggestive charms of the ruined city.

Macchu-Picchu is constructed on the top of a mountain, covering an area of some two kilometers in perimeter. It is basically divided into three sections: that of the two temples, another for the main residences and an area for the common people.

In the section reserved for religious activities are the ruins of a magnificent temple made of great, white granite blocks, with the three windows that gave rise to Bingham's mythological speculations. Adorning a series of beautifully constructed buildings is the Intiwatana, where the sun is moored: a stone finger some 60 centimeters high, the basis of indigenous rites and one of few such pieces still standing since the Spaniards were careful to destroy this symbol upon conquering any Inca fortress.

The buildings that housed the nobility show examples of extraordinary artistic value, for example the circular tower I have already mentioned, the sequence of bridges and canals cut into the stone and the many residences that are notable for the execution of their stonemasonry.

In the dwellings presumably occupied by the plebeians, one notes a great difference in the rough finish of the rock. They are separated from the religious part of the complex by a small square, or flat area, where the main water reservoirs — now dried up — were located, this supposedly being one of the main reasons for abandoning the place as a permanent residence.

Macchu-Picchu is a city of steps with almost all of its constructions on different levels, united by stairways, some of exquisitely carved rock, and others of stones aligned without much aesthetic zeal. But all of them, like the city as a whole, were capable of standing up to the rigors of the weather, and lost only their ceilings made of tree trunks and straw, unable to resist the assault of the elements.

Dietary needs were satisfied by vegetables planted in the terraces that are still perfectly conserved.

It was very easy to defend, surrounded on two sides by almost vertical slopes, a third passable only along readily defendable tracks, while the fourth faces Huaina-Picchu. This peak towers some 200 meters over its brother. It is difficult to climb, and would be almost impossible for the tourist, were it not for the remains of the Inca paving enabling one to edge to its peak along sheer precipices. The place seems to have been more for observation than anything else, since there are no major constructions. The River Urubamba encircles the two peaks almost completely, so they are almost impossible for attacking forces to take.

I have already noted that the archaeological meaning of Macchu-Picchu is disputed, but the origin of the city is not the vital thing and, in any case, it is best to leave the debate to specialists.

Most important and irrefutable is that here we have found the pure expression of the most powerful indigenous civilization in the Americas — still untainted by contact with conquering armies and replete with immensely evocative treasures between its walls that have died from the tedium of having no life among them. The spectacular landscape circling the fortress supplies an essential backdrop, inspiring dreamers to wander its ruins aimlessly; North American tourists, bound by their practical world view, are able to place those members of the disintegrating tribes they may have seen in their travels among these once-living walls, unaware of the moral distance between him and them, since only the semi-indigenous spirit of the South American can grasp the subtle differences.

Let us agree, for the moment, to give the city two possible meanings: one for the fighter, pursuing what is today described as chimeric, with an arm reaching toward the future and a stone voice crying out to be heard all over the continent, "Citizens of Indian-America, reconquer the past." And for others, those who would just be "far from the madding crowd," there are some appropriate words jotted down by a British subject in the hotel visitors' book, leaving in writing all the bitterness of imperial yearnings: "I am lucky to find a place without Coca-Cola propaganda."

Photograph taken by Ernesto Che Guevara.

thedilemmaofguatemala

Anyone who has traveled these lands of the Americas will have heard the disdainful pronouncements of some people about certain regimes with clearly democratic leanings. These sentiments date from the Spanish Republic and its fall. At that time they said the republic consisted of a mob of layabouts who knew only how to dance the *jota*, and that Franco established order and exiled communism from Spain. Time polished such opinions, standardizing criteria, and the words used, like stones thrown at any moribund democracy, went along the lines of, "That wasn't liberty there, but the rule of libertines."

The governments that in Peru, Venezuela and Cuba had held out the dream of a new era for the Americas were thus defined. The price that democratic groups in these countries have had to pay for their apprenticeship in the techniques of oppression has been high. A great number of innocent victims have been immolated to maintain an order required for the interests of the feudal bourgeoisie and foreign capital. Patriots now know that victory will have to be achieved by fire and sword, that there can be no forgiveness for traitors, and that the total extermination of reactionary groups is the only way to ensure the rule of justice in the Americas.

When I once again heard the words "rule of libertines" used to describe Guatemala, I feared for the small republic. Does it mean that the resurrection of the dream of the Latin American people, embodied by this country and by Bolivia, is condemned to go the way of its precursors? Herein lies the dilemma.

Four revolutionary parties constitute the support base of the government and all of them, except for the Guatemalan Workers' Party [PGT] are fragmented into two or more antagonistic factions that fight among themselves even more viciously than with their traditional feudal enemies, forgetting in their domestic squabbles the aspirations of the Guatemalan people. Meanwhile, the reactionary forces spread their nets wide. The U.S. State Department and the United Fruit Company — one never knows which is which in that country to the north — in open alliance with the landowners and the spineless, sanctimonious bourgeoisie — are making all kinds of plans to silence a proud adversary that has emerged for them like a pimple on the bosom of the Caribbean. While Caracas awaits orders that will open the way for more or less barefaced interference, the displaced little generals and the craven coffee growers seek to make alliances with other dictators in neighboring countries.

And while in the adjoining countries the fully muzzled press can only sing the praises of the "leader" on the only note permitted them, what pass for "independent" newspapers here unleash a farrago of long, involved stories about the government and its defenders, creating whatever climate they want. Democracy permits this. The "beachhead of communism," setting a magnificent example of freedom and ingenuity, permits them to undermine their own nationalist foundations, permits the destruction of yet another of Latin America's dreams.

Look back a little at the immediate past, *compañeros*, and observe the leaders who have had to flee, the murdered or imprisoned members of APRA [American Popular Revolutionary Alliance] in Peru, of Democratic Action in Venezuela, and look at the magnificent young Cubans assassinated by Batista. Draw close to the 20 bullet-wounds in the body of the poet soldier, Ruiz Pineda, and look at the miasmas of the Venezuelan prisons. Look fearlessly, but with care, at this past that serves as an example, and answer this question: is this the future of Guatemala?

Has the struggle been, is the struggle, for this? The historic responsibility of the men who must fulfill the hopes of Latin America is great. The time for euphemism is over. It is time that garrote answered garrote. If one must die, let it be like Sandino and not like Azaña.

May treacherous guns be grasped not in Guatemalan hands. If they want to kill freedom, let it be the other side who does it, those who hide freedom away. We must do away with softness; refuse to pardon treason. Let not the unshed blood of a traitor cost the lives of thousands of brave defenders of the people. The old dilemma of Hamlet has come to my lips, in the words of a poet from Guatemala-America: "Are you or are you not, or who are you?" Let the groups that support the government answer that.

If I present you with a landscape and say, for instance, that it was 'taken' at night, you can either believe me, or not; it matters little to me, since if you don't happen to know the scene I've 'photographed' in my notes, it will be hard for you to find an alternative to the truth I'm about to tell." Thus, the young Ernesto Guevara de la Serna, tireless traveler and conscious witness, warns the hypothetical reader about his notes.

In this section, which reveals three *ways of seeing*, we offer corroboration of his brash warning, along with a sampling of the diversity of his gaze. Here, the clear vision of the note-taker, the poet and the photographer come happily together to observe a single object: the ruins of Palenque.

Whatever views one might have about its quality, Ernesto Guevara's poetry is part of his observation, and while it stands in its own right, it surely remains today as yet one more example of his different modes of expression. Poetry accompanied him throughout his life, and was among the contents of his pack in his final mission as a guerrilla fighter. He read verses to his fellow fighters and engaged at a distance with the poets he loved, as we shall see later in this book. "Something lives on in your stone" is a warning from the young poet to the youth of this newly arrived 21st century. All one needs is to have one's eyes and ears open, to have one's sensibility beating in the left side of the chest, and to maintain a love that can multiply and extend all over the world.

—VC

04

three ways of seeing

palenque

The ruins of Palenque are magnificent. The nucleus of the city is on a hillside, and from the center it spreads over four to six kilometers into the middle of the forest. It is still unexplored, though the location of its constructions, which are covered with a tangle of plants, is well known.

The negligence of the authorities is total, so it took them three to four years to clean up the main tomb, one of the archaeological jewels of all the Americas. With the proper tools and people, they could have done it in three months. The principal buildings are the Palace, with its collection of galleries and patios, their stone engravings and stucco arrises, all highly artistic, and the Temple of the Inscriptions, also known as the Tomb, so called because its main feature is a burial place, the only one of its kind in Latin America. It is entered from the top of the pyramid, descending through a long tunnel with a trapezoidal roof, leading into a wide chamber where there is a monolithic tombstone 3.8 meters long, 2.2 meters wide and some 27 centimeters thick, adorned with hieroglyphics representing the sun, the moon and Venus. Beneath the tombstone is a catafalque, a single piece cut from a stone block, and this contains the body of some important figure.

There are jewels of different sizes, all worked in jade. Notable in Palenque are the beauty and redolence of its bas-reliefs and stuccowork, which were achieved with an art lost with the later advance of the dominions of the third millennium in which the Toltec influence was beginning to appear (with the work becoming more monumental and less sculptural).

The sculptural motifs of Palenque are more human than those of the Aztecs or Toltecs and generally depict whole-bodied human figures engaged in historic events or ritual proceedings together with the main gods of their Olympus: the sun, the moon, Venus, the god of the waters, etc.

Palenque, according to the classification of the U.S. archaeologist Morley, is a second-category center in the Mayan realm. (This archaeologist only concedes preeminent status to Copán, Tikal, Uxmal and Chichén-Itza). Archaeological research reveals that Palenque raised monuments in the first quarter of the ninth *baktún* (435–534), more or less contemporaneously with Piedras Negras, the other artistic center of the empire. All in all, there are 19 second-category cities in Morley's classification, although recent research is lending more significance to Palenque. Whether this city is first-category or not, most would find it undeniable that this is the city where Mayan stuccowork achieved the height of its technique and art.

palenque: something lives on in your stone

Something lives on in your stone,
sister of green dawning
and the silence of your ghosts
is a scandal to the tombs of kings.
Your heart is pierced by the indifferent pick
of some wise man in boring glasses
while your face is struck by the insolent offense
in the stupid "Oh!" of the gringo tourist.

But something in you is alive.

What it is I do not know
but the forest offers you the embrace of its trunks
and even the merciful scraping of its roots.
A huge zoologist wields the pin
with which to skewer your temples for the throne,
and still you do not die.

What force sustains you
beyond the centuries
live and throbbing as in your youth?
At the end of the day, what god blows
the breath of life into your stars?
Might it be the jocund tropical sun?
Why not in Chichén-Itza then?
Might it be the forest's jovial embrace
or the melodious song of birds?
And why is Quiriguá's sleep more sound?
Might it be the play of the melodious spring
beating in the roughness of the earth?
And yet, the Incas have died.

The epistolary writings of Ernesto Guevara always have been an essential component of his testimonial works, from the moment Che set out as a young traveler, discoverer of the lands of the Americas, a dreamer who revealed futures for us all with his perceptive gaze and intelligence. The significance of his letters was undiminished even once Che had matured, becoming Che the combatant and eventually Che the nation builder.

One day, the publication of Che's collected letters should be undertaken. However diverse their recipients and varied in their themes, these writings demonstrate the coherency of their author's thoughts. For the time being, this book offers two small selections. The first, "Letters from Afar," includes texts written in Central America (1953–54) and later from Mexico (1954–56).

Here we can trace the development of the young Ernesto and the definitive impact that this journey through Our America had on his personal and

political growth. Humor and irony, traits both integral to his personality and style, run freely through these letters in which Che confronts the opinions of his Aunt Beatriz, mocks the economic situation, recounts his work experiences and discovers for himself the truths that, years later, the world would come to admire: "The Americas will be the theater of my adventures, of much greater importance than I ever would have believed."

In addition to these letters, we have added fragments from his unfinished diary. With passion and perseverance, Che gathered in this diary notes about the many events that touched his life at that time.

The pace of events overtook Che, preventing him from returning to his notes to write a definitive version of his observations as he had done in *The Motorcycle Diaries*. The fragments we have included here, then, are the direct testimony of their author, written to the beat of the happenings they narrate.

Writing with such immediacy, Che's words reveal his great capacity for observation and analysis. This incorporates both the gaze he directs toward himself and his surroundings and the precision of his description as he provides a holistic and concise summary of facts and characters.

As the reader will note, there is also room for tenderness ("I feel a little like the good granddaddy"); for self-scrutiny, contradictory and therefore sincere ("Without doubt, I am an optimistic fatalist"); and for his contemplation of wider horizons ("Recent events belong to history…").

These notes reaffirm the analytical inclination of this witness who traveled widely, searched for truths and constructed an ethic which incorporated every moment of his existence. It is this ethic which allows Che to be reborn perpetually from his own ashes.

—VC

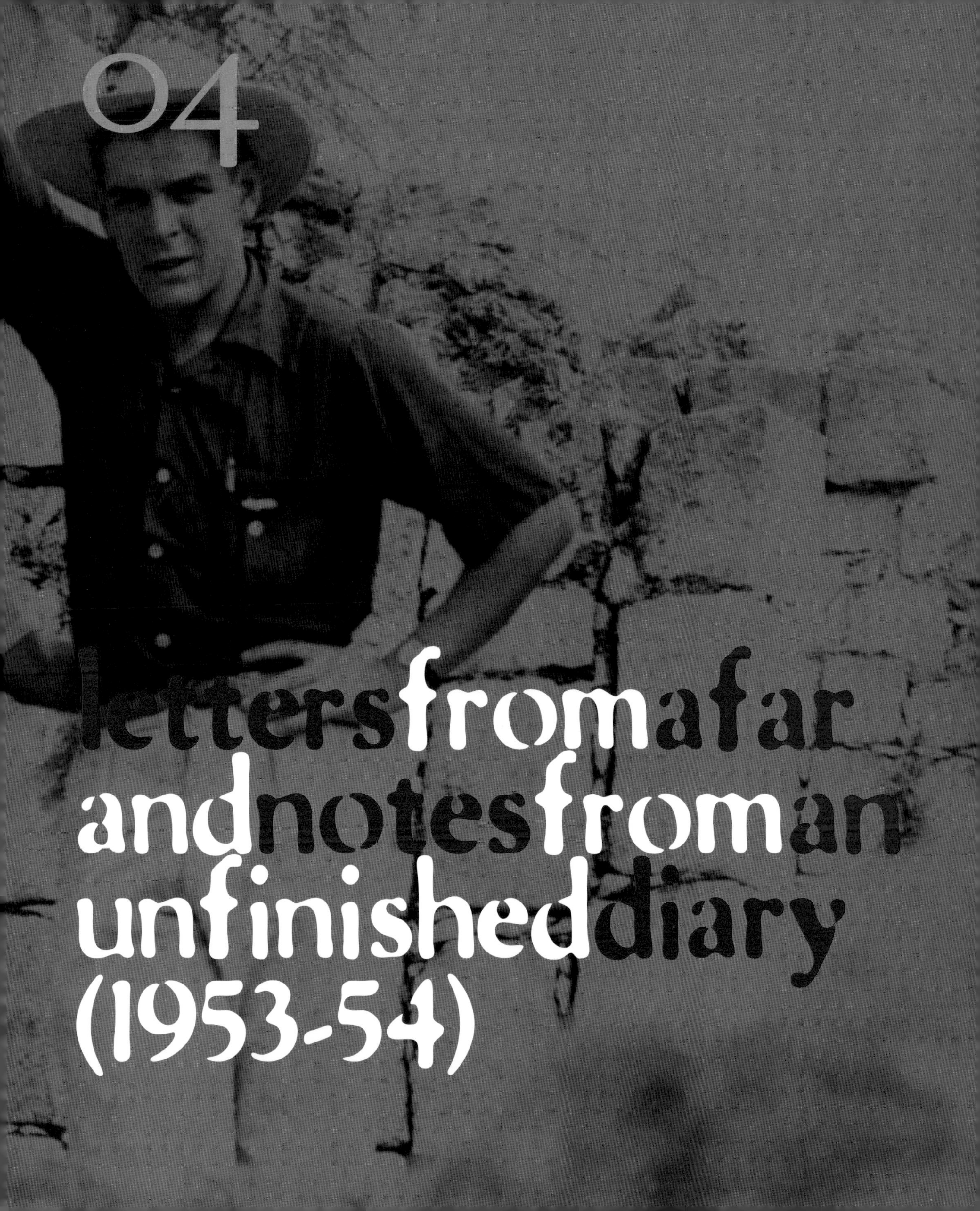

04

letters from afar
and notes from an
unfinished diary
(1953-54)

somelittleversesindeepred...

My dear Mamá,

You won't believe that this heading is to gladden Dad's heart, but there are signs that things are improving and the outlook is no longer so dire with regard to my economic prospects. I am telling you about the *peso* tragedy only because it happens to be true and I assumed that Dad would regard me as being tough enough to take what comes. If you prefer fairytales, however, the ones I can tell are very beautiful. In these days of silence, the events of my life have been thus: I went with a pack and a briefcase, half walking, half hitching, only half (to my shame) paying my way, thanks to the $10 the government itself had given me. I reached Salvador and the police confiscated some books I was bringing from Guatemala, but I got through and managed to obtain a visa to return to the latter. With everything sorted out, I set about visiting the ruins of the *pipiles*, a race of Tlascaltecs that set out to conquer the south (their center was in Mexico) and here they remained until the Spaniards came. They have nothing to do with Mayan constructions, and still less with the Incan.

Then I went and spent a few days at the beach while waiting for my visa to come through. I had asked for it in order to visit some splendid Honduran ruins. I spent the nights by the sea, in a sleeping bag I have acquired, and, though my diet was not totally strict, I was in fine form from this healthy life, except for some sunburn. I befriended some Chochamu who, like everyone in Central America, are good drinkers, gave them my piece of Guatemalan propaganda and recited some little verses in deep red. The result: we all ended up in the slammer, but they let us out at once after a word of advice from a commander, who seemed a fine fellow, who suggested that I sing to the afternoon roses and other things of beauty. I preferred to compose a sonnet for him on the vanishing quality of smoke. The Hondurans denied me a visa for the simple fact of my living in Guatemala although, needless to say, it was my healthy intention to have a look at a strike that has taken off there with the support of 25 percent of the entire working population, a high figure anywhere but extraordinary in a country where there is no right to strike and the unions must organize clandestinely. The fruit company is furious and of course Dulles and C(IA)o want to intervene in Guatemala because of its terrible crime of buying arms on whatever market it could because the United States hasn't sold them as much as a single cartridge for a long time...

Naturally I didn't consider the possibility of staying there. On the way back, I headed off on semi-abandoned roads with my wallet in a terrible state because here a dollar is worth about one mango*, so even 20 doesn't go very far. Some days I walked about 50 kilometers (maybe that's stretching it a bit, but a lot anyway) and, after many days, I arrived at the fruit company hospital where there is a complex of small but very beautiful ruins. There I became totally convinced of what my Latin American blood did not want to acknowledge: that our forbears are Asian (tell the old man that soon they are going to strip him of his paternal authority). There are figures in bas-relief that are Buddha himself, all the details show it, for they are exactly the same as in the ancient Hindu civilizations. The place is really beautiful, so much so that I committed Silvestre Bonard's crime against my stomach and spent a dollar and a bit to buy film and hire myself a camera. Then I begged a bite to eat at the hospital but didn't even manage to get the hump half full. I had no money to get to Guatemala by train so I headed off for Puerto Barrios where I labored away unloading barrels of tar, earning $2.63 an hour for 12 hours, working as hard as hell in a place where there are ravenous mosquitoes diving at you in astonishing numbers. My hands finished up in a terrible state and my back was worse, but I confess that I was quite happy. I worked from six in the afternoon till six in the morning and slept in an abandoned house by the sea. Then I left for Guatemala and here I am with better prospects...

...(this writing isn't really my own outlandish thoughts but rather the influence of four Cubans arguing right next to me)...

Next time, when things are a bit quieter I'll send you any news I have...

Love to all.

* Argentine slang for *peso*.

iamanoptimisticfatalist...

...Nine days to bring together in my diary notes. Days full of inner life and nothing else. A collection of all kinds of failures and the unchanging spiral of hopes. There is no doubt about it, I am an optimistic fatalist. I've had asthma these days, the last few confined to my room hardly going out at all, although yesterday we went with the Venezuelans and Nicanor Mújica to Amatitlán. There, they got into a heavy argument, all of them against me, except for fat Rojo who stated that I do not have the moral quality to engage in the debate. Today I went to see about the possibilities of working as a doctor for 80 a month for one hour's work a day. In the IGSS [Guatemala Institute of Social Security] they told me with utmost certainty that there are no positions. Solórzano was friendly and concise. Now the day can come to an end with the old full stop. We shall see.

my life has been a sea of conflicting decisions...

December 10, 1953
San José de Costa Rica

Auntie-auntie-mine [Beatriz],

My life has been a sea of conflicting decisions until I bravely abandoned my baggage and, pack on my back, set off with my *compañero* García on the winding road that has led us here. In El Paso, I had the chance to travel through the realms of United Fruit, which once again convinced me of how terrible these capitalist octopuses are. I have sworn before a picture of the old and late-lamented Stalin not to rest until I see these capitalist octopuses wiped out. In Guatemala I shall hone myself and do what I have to do to become a true revolutionary.

I must tell you that, apart from being a doctor, I am also a journalist and lecturer, activities which bring (though only a few) $US.

Along with all the rest, hugs, kisses and love from your nephew, he of the iron constitution, empty stomach and shining faith in a socialist future.

Bye,
Chancho*

* Argentine Spanish for pig.

evenaskepticlikeme...

...I shall have to succeed without means and I believe I'll do it, but I also think that success will be more as the result of my natural qualities — which are greater than my subconscious would believe — than the faith I have in doing so. When I heard the Cubans making their grandiloquent assertions with total serenity, I felt like a little kid. I can give a speech that is 10 times more objective and without the platitudes, can do it better and can convince an audience that what I am saying is true. The difference is, I don't convince myself and the Cubans do. Nico left his soul in the microphone, firing even a skeptic like me with enthusiasm....

thetwomesthatbattle inside,thesocialreformer andthetraveler...

May 10, 1954

Dear old Mamá,

...Apart from still looking to a poverty-flavored future, my permission for residence is advancing, though with all the red tape characterizing these parts, and I suppose that within a month I'll be able to go see a film without sponging off some kind neighbor.

I have promised myself something I think I already told the old man, and I also gave him a vague idea of my projects. I have decided to leave these lodgings on May 15 and head off into the open air with a sleeping bag I inherited from a compatriot who was passing through here. That way, I can get to know all the places I want except Petén, where you can't go because it's the rainy season, and I'll be able to climb a volcano or two. For some time now, I've been wanting to take a look at Mother Earth's tonsils (what a nice turn of phrase). This is the land of volcanoes to satisfy every taste, and the ones I like are the simple ones, not very high and not very active. I could get very rich in Guatemala, but only after putting myself through the abject business of ratifying my degree, setting up a clinic and treating allergies (the place is full of fellow snufflers).

Doing this would be the most horrible betrayal of the two mes that battle inside, the social reformer and the traveler...

Warm and damp hugs because it's been raining here all day (while the *mate* lasts, it's very romantic).

With friends, attempting to scale
Mt Popocatepetl, Mexico.

Che with Hilda Gadea, 1955.

recent events belong to history...

...Recent events belong to history: a quality, I think, appearing in my notes for the first time.

A few days ago, some planes from Honduras crossed the border with Guatemala and flew over the city, in broad daylight, shooting both people and military targets. I joined with the public health brigades to work in the medical section and with the youth brigades that patrol the streets at night. The course of events was as follows: after these planes flew over, troops under the command of Colonel Castillo Armas, a Guatemalan emigré to Honduras, crossed the border and advanced on the town of Chiquimula. The Guatemalan Government, although it had already protested to Honduras, let them enter without putting up any resistance and presented the case before the United Nations.

Colombia and Brazil, docile Yankee instruments, drew up a project to hand the matter over to the OAS [Organization of American States] but this was rejected by the Soviet Union, which favored a ceasefire agreement. The invaders failed in their attempt to get the masses to rise up in arms, which they had dropped from planes, but they did capture the population of the banana estates and cut off the Puerto Barrios railway line.

The goal of the mercenaries was clear: take Puerto Barrios and then ship in various arms and further mercenary troops. This became clear when the schooner *Siesta de Trujillo* was captured as it tried to offload arms in the port. The final attack failed but in the hinterland areas the assailants committed extremely barbarous acts, murdering members of SETUFCO (the union of the United Fruit workers and employees) in the cemetery, where hand grenades were thrown at their chests.

The invaders believed that they only had to say the word and the people would rise up as one to follow them, and that's why they parachute-dropped weapons, but the people immediately put themselves at Arbenz's orders. Though the invading troops were blocked and defeated on all fronts until they were pushed back beyond Chiquimula near the Honduran border, the planes kept attacking the battlefronts and towns, always coming from Honduran and Nicaraguan bases. Chiquimula was heavily bombed and bombs also fell on Guatemala City, injuring several people and killing a little girl of three.

My own activities were as follows: first I presented myself at the premises of the youth brigades of the alliance where we stayed together for several days until the minister of public health sent me to a clinic, which is in the teacher's house in the zone where I am billeted. I tried to sign up as a volunteer to go to the front but they wouldn't even look at me. Today, Saturday, June 26, the minister came, but I had gone to see Hilda and was furious because I wanted to ask him to send me to the front...

my position is in no way that of a dilettante full of hot air…

February 12, 1954

My very dear, always adored and never duly praised aunt [Beatriz],

I was really pleased to receive your last letter, the culmination and complement of the two previous "capitalists"* of which I only received one, meaning that the democratic post office employee was dishing out a just distribution of wealth.

Don't send me any more money as it will cost you all the silver in Peru. I can find all the dollar bills I need here paving the ground, and I can tell you I ended up with lumbago after so much bending over to pick them up at the beginning. Now I only take one in every 10, just to maintain public hygiene standards because so much paper flying about and on the ground is a danger.

My plan for the coming years: at least six months in Guatemala, if I don't find anything that is well enough paid to permit me to stay for two years. In the first case, I'll go and work in another country for a year, which might mean, in diminishing order of probability, Venezuela, Mexico, Cuba and the United States.

If the two-year plan comes off, after a visit to the three latter countries, along with Haiti and Santo Domingo, I'm off to Western Europe, where I'll stay until I've blown the final monetary cartridge. If there's time and cash in the meantime, I'll come and pay you a visit by some bargain-basement means, a free flight or boat or working as a doctor.

In this general plan, there are two highly changeable factors that could pull things one way or the other. The first is money, which, for me, is not of primary importance, but it does cut short stays and modify itineraries, etc. The second and more important is the political situation. MY POSITION IS IN NO WAY THAT OF A DILETTANTE FULL OF HOT AIR AND NOTHING ELSE. I HAVE TAKEN A DETERMINED POSITION IN SUPPORT OF THE GUATEMALAN GOVERNMENT AND WITHIN IT, IN THE PGT GROUP, WHICH IS COMMUNIST. I ALSO HAVE CONNECTIONS WITH SOME INTELLECTUALS OF THESE LEANINGS WHO BRING OUT A MAGAZINE HERE, AND I WORK AS A DOCTOR IN THE UNIONS. THIS HAS PUT ME AT LOGGERHEADS WITH THE TOTALLY REACTIONARY MEDICAL COLLEGE. I can imagine everything you will have to say and remark upon at this point, but at least you can't complain about me not being frank.

In the field of social medicine, and on the basis of my limited personal experience, I am working on a very pretentious book, which I think will take me two years' work. It is called *El función del médico en América Latina* (The Role of the Doctor in Latin America) and, so far, I only have the general plan and the first two chapters written. I think that, with a bit of patience and methodology, I can say something good.

A fearless hug from your proletarian nephew.

Important P.S.: Tell me what you're thinking of doing with the apartment and if it's possible to send books for you to keep. Don't worry, they aren't compromising.

* Word play between *capítulo* (chapter) and *capitalista* (capitalist).

ihavebeenrenamed "chebol" andtherepressioniscoming...

...Two days dense with political events, although they have not affected me much personally. The events have been: Arbenz steps down under pressure from a U.S. military mission threatening massive bombing attacks, and a declaration of war from Honduras and Nicaragua, which would lead to the United States becoming involved. What Arbenz possibly did not foresee was what came next. The first day, colonels Sánchez and Fejo Monsón, both avowedly anticommunist, pledged their support for Díaz and the first decree was to outlaw the PGT. The persecution began immediately and the embassies filled up with asylum seekers, but the worst came early the next day when Díaz and Sánchez stepped aside, leaving Monsón at the head of the government with the two lieutenant colonels as his subordinates. *Vox populi* has it that they totally gave themselves over to Castillo Armas and martial law was declared as a measure against anyone that might be found bearing any arms of prohibited caliber. My personal situation is more or less this: I'll be expelled from the little hospital where I am now, probably tomorrow, because I have been renamed "Chebol"* and the repression is coming.

* Che (a common Argentine form of address) plus Bol(shevik).

portraits

(Guatemala)

...Several days have gone by without any milestones to mark my stay in the embassy. The government of Castillo Armas is now completely consolidated. Several prisoners were taken from military ranks and that was it. My cohabitation with a number of people who sleep under the same roof in the embassy leads me to offer a superficial analysis of each one...

Roberto Castañeda: Guatemalan, a photographer by profession though he doesn't shine much there, and he's also a dancer. He gives me the impression of somebody with an artistic temperament, clear intelligence and a perfectionist zeal in everything he does. He has traveled behind the Iron Curtain and is a sincere admirer of it although he did not join the party. He lacks theoretical knowledge of Marxism and perhaps wouldn't make a good militant because of these bourgeois flaws, shall we say, but there is no doubt that the moment the action starts he'll be with us. He strikes me as a wonderful character for his style of relationships, and he has practically none of the dancer's effeminacy...

Luis Arturo Pineda: Guatemalan, 21 years old, member of the PGT. He's a serious lad, proud of his militancy and a firm believer in the infallibility of the party, so that his highest aspirations are to be secretary of the party in Guatemala, or in Latin America maybe, and to shake hands with Malenkov. From the heights of his militant orthodoxy he looks with disdain upon anything that is not subject to party discipline. He regards himself as very intelligent but he isn't, though he's by no means a fool. His militancy leads him to make any kind of sacrifice for the party...

Ricardo Ramírez is perhaps one of the most able youth leaders. Evidently the party for him is a substitute for a home, which he appears not to have had in his youth or, to be more precise, his childhood, because he's just turned 23. He's going to Buenos Aires where it is clear that the experience in the party will do him good. He's highly cultured and his way of confronting problems is much less dogmatic than that of other comrades...

Humberto Pineda is perhaps the leader recognized by us all and by the embassy. He is a man who has given up his violent impulses, as have his sons, in favor of reason and calm. His intellectual capacity is not that great and neither is his intellectual training, but he can handle anything that is expected of him and is a good militant.

This page: In Mexico.

theamericaswillbethe
theaterofmyadventures...

Guatemala, April 1954

Dear *vieja*,*

...I'm happy that you have such a high opinion of me. In any case, it is very unlikely that archaeology would be the exclusive concern of my mature years. It seems somewhat paradoxical to me that I should make my life's "guiding star" the study of what is irremediably dead. I am certain of two things: first is that if I get to my truly creative phase at about 35 years, my exclusive, or at least main, concern will be nuclear physics, or genetics, or some other field that brings together the most interesting aspects of knowledge, and second is that the Americas will be the theater of my adventures in a way that is much more significant than I would have believed. I really think I have come to understand her, and I feel Latin American in a way that is different from the way I feel about any other place on earth. Naturally, I will travel the rest of the world...

* *Vieja*, or old woman, a common affectionate form of addressing mothers.

"The first stage of the great adventure has concluded happily, and here I am installed in Mexico, although I have no idea about the future," wrote Ernesto in his notes, in mid-September 1954.

In the pages of this vivid and instructive diary, we are still finding keys to understanding the life of its chronicler — topics to which Ernesto returns time and again in his notes: the battle for survival in the new city, professional photography as a source of income, and his interest in scientific matters, especially those related to medicine.

In the midst of this "routine chain of hopes and disappointments characterizing my proletarian life," Ernesto reviews what he has lived and learned in his letters to his parents and his aunt. More than his reading and incessant study of philosophy, history and literature, the insights which Latin America granted Ernesto on his adventure-pilgrimage sharpened his vision and directed his path to that zone of personal commitment which makes millions marvel even today.

The balance of Ernesto's experiences in Guatemala are doubtless a landmark in his endless process of interrogating reality and actively seeking his own transformation.

Mexico was home to important events in Ernesto's personal life, such as the birth of his first child Hildita. He comments in a letter at the time, with the jubilation and curiosity borne from his new role as a father, "Now I'll tell you about the kid."

A determined explorer of the world around him, challenging his own strength of will in every situation and climate, Ernesto was one of a group of friends who took on the peak of Popocatepetl: a metaphor, perhaps, of the greater undertakings of his life and of the constant tension between his will and the challenges he decided to accept.

The first meetings in Guatemala with the Cuban revolutionaries, though he didn't know it yet, would launch Ernesto on to a new path of searching, investigation and adventure. This possibility became more concrete in Mexico, with a fact noted rapidly in the pages of Ernesto's diary: "One political event is meeting Fidel Castro, the Cuban revolutionary, an intelligent young man who is very sure of himself and extraordinarily bold; I think we like each other."

Largely through Che's letters we can reconstruct, visualize or imagine — depending on the case — the complexity which the young Ernesto was encountering. If we are able to follow the formation of his political ideas, his concrete political knowledge, his doubts and his certainties, it is thanks to his letters. Commenting, clarifying, rebutting the criticism of those he dearly loved — such as his mother — Ernesto scratched his lines between solitude, momentary disappointments and emerging convictions in his unfinished diary.

It is from these writings that we know that the young Ernesto Guevara de la Serna, impenitent traveler, seeker of landscape, vocation and destiny, found himself at a turning point: the needle on the scales began to tip toward the history of the years ahead.

Che's word as a witness announces this changing direction amid daily anecdotes: "Five jobs I was offered fell through, so I signed up as a photographer in a small company and my progress in the cinematic arts is rapid. My plans for the future are unclear but I hope to finish a couple of research tasks. This year could be important for my future. I've already left the hospitals. I'll write soon with more details."

That year would see him embark for a new land, Cuba, where adventure and the struggle for Our America were beginning to take a new and more hopeful shape.

—VC

04

letters from afar and notes from an unfinished diary (mexico 1954-56)

I'm installed in mexico...

...The first stage of the great adventure has concluded happily, and here I'm installed in Mexico, although I have no idea about the future. I left [Guatemala], accompanied by my little doubts, till I got to the border; getting through was cheap but the professional swindlers began on the Mexican side. I joined up with a good lad from Guatemala to get in, an engineering student named Julio Roberto Cáceres Valle, who also seems under the sway of this obsession for traveling. I'm thinking of moving on to Veracruz to try to take the great leap there.

We did the trip to Mexico together but now I am alone here. Maybe [...] will come back.

asfortheu.s.a.ihaven't lostanounceoffight...

November 1954

Vieja, my *vieja*,

(I confused you with the date)

...To tell you about my life is to repeat myself because I'm not doing anything new. Photography is bringing in enough to live on and there are no really well-founded hopes that I might be able to leave it in the near future, although I'm working every morning researching in two hospitals. I think the best thing that could happen to me would be to slip into a job as a country doctor in the informal sector, somewhere very near the capital, making it easier to devote my time to medicine for some months. I'm doing this because, now that I'm comparing notes with people who've studied in the United States and who are no fools with regard to orthodox knowledge, I'm perfectly aware of how much I learned about allergies with Pisani. I think Pisani's method is light years better, so I want to get practise with all the ins and outs of his systems and then I can land on my feet wherever it may be...

I'm slaving away here, busy every morning in the hospital and in the afternoons and Sundays I work as a photographer, while at night I study a bit. I think I told you that I'm in a good apartment, I cook my own food and do everything myself, as well as bathing every day thanks to the fact I can use as much hot water as I like.

As you can see, I'm changing in this aspect, but otherwise I'm the same because I don't wash my clothes very often, and wash them badly when I do, and I still don't earn enough to pay a laundry.

The scholarship is a dream I've given up on, as it seems that in such a large country as this you don't ask; you just do your thing and that's it. You know that I have always been inclined to make drastic decisions, and here the pay is great. Everyone is lazy, but they don't get in the way when other people get things done, so I've got free rein either here or in the country where I might go. Naturally, this doesn't make me lose sight of my goal, which is Europe, where I'm planning to go no matter what happens.

As for the U.S.A., I haven't lost an ounce of fight, but I still want to get a good idea of New York, at least. I'm not in the least worried about what might happen and know that I'll come out of it as anti-Yankee as I go in (that's if I do get in).

I'm happy that people are waking up a bit, although I don't know what guides them in doing so. But anyway, the truth is that Argentina is as insipid as you can get even though in general terms the picture we get here from outside seems to suggest that they are taking notable strides forward and that the country will be perfectly able to defend itself from the crises that the Yankees are about to set off by dumping their surplus food...

Communists don't have your sense of friendship but, among themselves, it is the same or better than yours. I have seen this very clearly and, in the disaster of Guatemala after the government was overthrown and it was every man for himself, the communists remained intact in their faith and comradeship and they constitute the only group that continued working there.

I think they are worthy of respect and that sooner or later I'll join the party, but what mainly stops me from doing so, for the moment, is that I'm mad to travel around Europe and I couldn't do this if I submitted to such rigorous discipline.

Vieja, till Paris.

theroutinechainofhopes anddisappointments characterizingmy proletarianlife...

...The days have gone by with the routine chain of hopes and disappointments characterizing my proletarian life. The stand at the book fair was a dream that is now over but now I have something new and nicer, though equally insecure: the boss of Agencia Latina offered me a job in which I'd earn 500 *pesos* a month working three times a week writing up journalistic syntheses of events in Mexico. For the moment I'm continuing as a photographer but am increasingly less inclined to do so. The idea of going it alone is floating in the air but we need cash.

thejourneywasquitelong andthereweremany backwardsteps...

[Mexico, end of 1954]

Vieja, my *vieja*,

With regard to the differences of opinion that you think you accentuated, I promise you that it will only be for a short time. What you are so afraid of can be reached by two roads: the positive one, when you convince someone directly, or the negative one, by way of disillusionment with everything. I came along the second path, only to be immediately convinced that it is essential to follow the first. The way that the gringos treat Latin America (remember that gringos are Yankees) was making me feel increasingly indignant, but at the same time I studied the reasons for their actions and found them scientific.

Afterwards, there was Guatemala. That is all difficult to recount, to see how the object of one's enthusiasm was diluted by the will of those gentlemen, and how the new tale of red guilt and criminality was already being forged, and how the same treacherous Guatemalans set about propagating the story to get some crumbs from under the table of the new order of things. I can't tell you the precise moment I put reasoning aside and acquired something like faith, not even approximately, as the journey was quite long and there were many backward steps.

ithinkwelike eachother...

...One political event is meeting Fidel Castro, the Cuban revolutionary, an intelligent young fellow who is very sure of himself and extraordinarily bold; I think we like each other...

i'llletyouhaveanaccount ofthematter…

Mexico, June 6, 1956, State penitentiary

Dear parents,

I received your letter (Dad) here in my new and exquisite mansion of Miguel Schultz, along with a visit from Petit who informed me of your fears. To give you an idea, I'll let you have an account of the matter.

Some time ago, quite a while ago, a young Cuban leader invited me to join his movement, a movement for the armed liberation of his country and, naturally, I accepted. In my work of providing some physical training for the bunch of kids that will be setting foot in Cuba some day, I spent the last months keeping this up under cover of being a teacher. On June 21 (when I had been away from my home in Mexico City because I was at a ranch on the outskirts), Fidel was arrested with a group of comrades and the address we were staying at was found in the house, so we all fell into the net. I had with me documents accrediting me as a student of Russian, which was enough for them to regard me as an important link in the organization, and the news agencies that Dad admires so much began to bellow all around the world.

This is a synthesis of what's been happening in the past; the future falls into two categories, the medium term and the immediate. As for the medium term, let me tell you now that my future is joined to that of the Cuban Revolution. Either triumph with it or die there. (This explains the somewhat enigmatic and romantic letter I sent to Argentina some time ago.) As for the immediate future, I have little to say because I don't know what is to become of me. I am in the judge's hands and it will be easy for them to deport me to Argentina unless I manage to obtain exile in some intermediate country, which I consider would be good for my political health.

In any case, I have to leave for my new destination, stay in this prison or leave it a free man. Hilda will go back to Peru, which now has a new government and has declared a political amnesty.

For obvious reasons, there'll be less correspondence from me from now on and, besides, the Mexican police have the charming habit of confiscating letters, so don't write about anything except family matters or banalities. Give Beatriz a kiss and tell her why I'm not writing and not to worry about sending newspapers for the moment.

We're about to declare an indefinite hunger strike because of the unjustified detentions and the torture to which some of my companions were submitted. Group morale is high.

For the moment, keep writing to me at home.

If for any reason I think that I won't be able to write anymore, and then I end up among the losers, consider these lines as my farewell, maybe not very grandiloquent but sincere.

I have spent my life stumbling about seeking my own truth and somewhere along the way, with a daughter to perpetuate me, I have closed the cycle. From now on, I wouldn't consider my death as a frustration, or only in the sense that Hikmet did: "I'll go to my grave regretting nothing but an unfinished song."

Kisses for all,
from Ernesto

Above: At the Miguel E. Schultz 136 prison, Mexico, 1956.

todayifeellikethe
goodgranddaddy...

...Today I feel like the good granddaddy who deals out good advice; Patojo went off to Guatemala with a "bastard" brother of his. This was the result of a conversation in which I said he was running away from something, and not fighting, as he was claiming in a letter to his mother that he read me; the next day he decided to leave, and a little later his brother went off to be with him.

Besides the cash he'd lent me earlier, I gave him $150 more, which Piaza lent me. My situation is strange because I'm counting on the salary of the Agencia Latina and they keep stringing me along with very vague promises. In the scientific field, I have great hopes, but reality's not letting me do anything about them yet. I started studying the process of doing electrophoresis with filter paper, and hope to start working with it in one or two weeks. I'm writing home very little so I don't know much of what's happening there.

foranygreatwork passionisneeded...

I'm no Christ or philanthropist, *vieja*. I'm exactly the opposite of a Christ and philanthropy looks [illegible] to me, but for what I believe in, I fight with all the weapons within my reach, and I try to lay out the other guy instead of letting myself get nailed to a cross or anywhere else. As for the hunger strike, you are totally wrong: we started it twice and the first time they freed 21 of the 24 detainees; the second time they announced that they would free Fidel Castro, the head of the movement, which will happen tomorrow, and if they do as they say, only two of us will be left in prison. I don't want you to believe, as Hilda hints, that the two of us who are left have been sacrificed. We are simply the ones whose papers aren't in order and so we can't avail ourselves of the conditions that our comrades could. My projects are to leave for the nearest country that will give me asylum, which could be difficult given the inter-American fame they have lumbered me with, and to prepare myself there for when my services will be necessary. I'm telling you yet again that it is likely I won't be able to write for a more or less longish period.

What really destroys me is your lack of understanding about all this and your advice about moderation, self-centeredness, etc., which in other words are the most execrable qualities an individual could have. Not only am I not moderate, I shall try never to be so, and when I recognize in myself that the holy flame has become a timid little votive light, the least I can do is to start vomiting on my own shit. As for your recommending moderate self-centeredness, which is to say crude and spineless individualism, I must tell you that I've done a lot to abolish such 20th century virtues in myself. I don't mean so much the former, this craven type whom I don't know, but the other one, the bohemian, unconcerned about his neighbor, with a sense of self-sufficiency because of an awareness, mistaken or otherwise, of his own strength. In these days in prison, and in the earlier days of training, I totally identified with my comrades-in-arms. I recall some words that I once thought were imbecile, or at least strange, with regard to such total identification between the members of a group of combatants, to the effect that the idea of "I" had completely given way to that of "we." It was a communist principle and naturally it might look like doctrinaire exaggeration but it was (and is) really beautiful to feel this rejection of the I for the we.

(The splotches aren't tears of blood but tomato juice.)

You are profoundly wrong to believe that moderation or "moderate self-centeredness" gives rise to great inventions or works of art. For any great work passion is needed, and boldness in large doses, and these qualities we have as human beings in general. Another strange thing that I note about you is your repeated citing of Daddy God, so I hope you're not reverting to the sheepfold of your youth. I can also warn you that the SOSs you sent out are to no avail: Petit shat himself, Lezica dodged the issue and (against my orders) gave Hilda a sermon on the obligations of political exile. Raúl Lynch behaved well at a distance, and Padilla Nervio said they were from different ministries. They could all help but only on condition that I forsake my ideals and I don't think you would prefer to have a living son who was a Barabbas rather than a son who died in whatever place doing what he considered as his duty. These attempts to help only put pressure on them and on me.

Again, there's no doubt that, after righting the wrongs in Cuba, I'll go anywhere at all, and it's also for sure that, locked up in some office of bureaucrats or some clinic of allergic ailments, I'd be fucked. All in all, I think that this pain, the pain of a mother who's getting old and wants her son alive, is a respectable thing and I must attend to it, and more than that, I want to attend to it. I would like to see you, not just to console you, but also to console myself in my sporadic and shameful homesickness.

A kiss for you, *vieja*, and a promise to come to see you if nothing else happens.

From your son, CHE.

i'mafather...

...A long time has gone by and many events have not been announced.
I'll just tell you about the most important. Since February 15, 1956,
I've been a father: Hilda Beatriz Guevara is my firstborn.

nowi'lltellyou aboutthekid...

Dear Mamá,

...I'd even lost the habit of writing but I've convinced myself, too, that it's the only way of getting news from the top circles of Buenos Aires...

Now I'll tell you about the kid: I'm very happy with her. My communist soul is bursting with joy — she's just like Mao Zedong. You can already see the incipient baldness in the middle of her nut, the kindly eyes of the leader and the protuberant jowls. For the moment she weighs less than five kilos but with time that will balance out. She's more spoiled than most children and eats the way I used to, at least according to her grandmother's tales: in other words, she sucks away without breathing until the milk comes out of her nose.

on arm, the fantasy...

year be future...

[circa October 1956]

Dear Mamá,

...As you'll recall, and if you don't remember I'll remind you now, I was working on a book on the role of the doctor, etc., of which I only finished a couple of chapters that whiffed of some pamphlet with a title like *Bodies and Souls*. They were nothing more than badly written rubbish, showing with every step a thorough ignorance of the basics of the topic, so I decided to study. Again, to write it, I had to reach a series of conclusions that were kicking against my essentially adventurous trajectory, so I decided to deal with the main things first, to pit myself against the order of things, shield on my arm, the whole fantasy, and then, if the windmills don't break open my head, write more later.

Another kiss for you, with all the love of a farewell that still resists being total.

Your son.

Five jobs I was offered fell through, so I signed up as a photographer in a small company and my progress in the cinematic arts is rapid. My plans for the future are unclear but I hope to finish a couple of research tasks. This year could be important for my future. I've already left the hospitals. I'll write soon with more details.

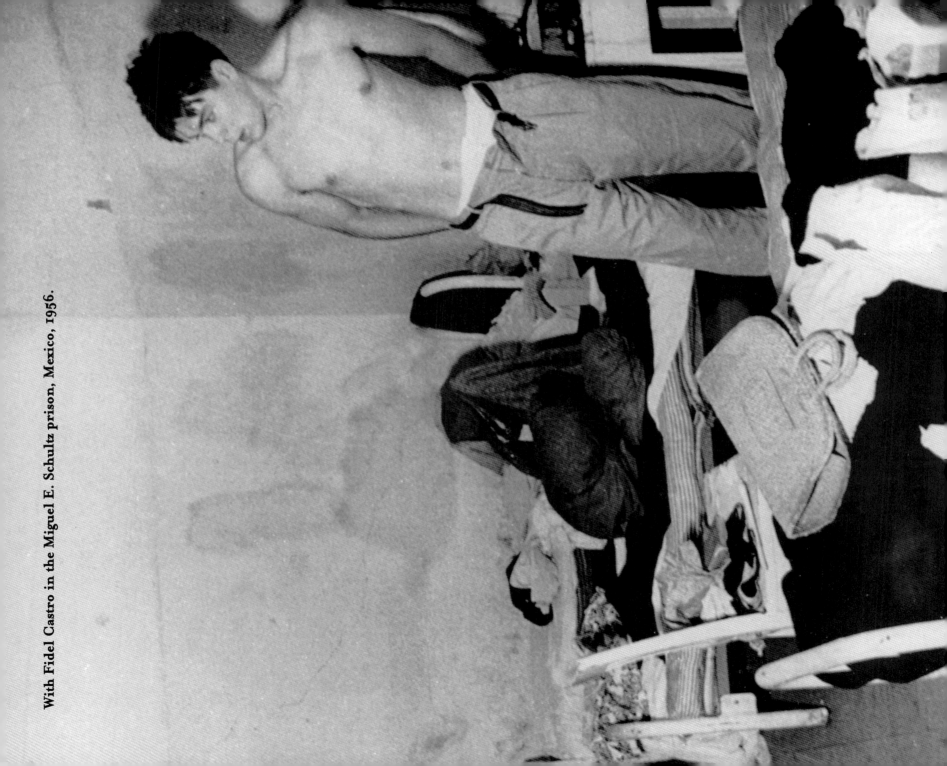

With Fidel Castro in the Miguel E. Schultz prison, Mexico, 1956.

Ernesto Guevara reconfirms his vocation as witness in the Sierra Maestra. In Mexico, during the preparations for the liberation war, his Cuban comrades gave him a new name that would accompany him through his future work and battles: Che. Here, however, in the pages of *El Cubano Libre*, a newspaper that continues the tradition of the 19th century Cuban revolutionary press, he writes under the pen name of Francotirador (Sharpshooter).

These brief commentaries are not yet the episodes of the revolutionary war which appeared in the pages of the periodical *Verde Olivo* after the triumph of 1959, and which came to light again in 1963, this time in book form as published by Ediciones Unión.

These articles for the newspaper's column "Sin bala en el directo" (With an unloaded gun), written quickly, amid the pressure of war and with immediate informative and ideological aims, touch on two distinct themes that are united by the sharp humor and ironic efficacy of the author.

The man writing these urgent notes for the rebel press is, and yet is not, the same itinerant Latin American. He has identified his route now, while maintaining his capacity for investigation and analysis, which will subsequently take him off to other lands, other exploits and other combats.

Ever present is the value he places on friendship, now forged and strengthened in combat: we have his portrait of Ciro Redondo, hitherto unpublished. There is also the biting edge of his humor, revealed in an interview in the Sierra Maestra conducted by the journalist Jorge Ricardo Masetti, "the first compatriot I've seen in ages."

The Murdered Puppy, his story that was later included in *Episodes from the Revolutionary War*, shows a vigorous and sensitive writer at work, capable of preserving a tenderness in his anecdotes of daily life.

—VC

chronicles fromthesierra maestra

putyourtrust ingodbeing argentine...

Sra. Celia de la Serna
Araoz 2180
Buenos Aires, Argentina

Dear parents,

I'm fine, two down and five to go.*

I'm still working at the same thing. News is sporadic and will continue to be so, but put your trust in God being Argentine.

A big hug to you all.

Teté**

* In Spanish a cat has seven lives, not nine.

** Che's pseudonym in Cuba was Teté Calvache.

Right: Days of freedom. With combatant Aleida March. Santa Clara, Cuba, 1958.

our soul is filled with compassion

with an unloaded gun, by sharpshooter

The society for the protection of animals paraded six dogs before the UN building seeking clemency for their Siberian relative Laika, the dog that is flying in astral spaces.

Our soul is filled with compassion to think of the poor animal that will die gloriously in honor of a cause it does not understand.

But we have not heard that any philanthropic society in the United States is parading in front of that noble building to plead clemency for our peasants, and they are dying in considerable numbers, machine-gunned by P-47 and B-26 aircraft, destroyed by shelling or riddled with bullets from the troops' M-15s.

Do the members of philanthropic societies know that these deaths are caused by arms supplied by their compatriots in the U.S. Government?

Or is it that, in the framework of political expediency, the life of a Siberian dog is worth more than those of a thousand Cuban peasants?

a biographical sketch of ciro

with an unloaded gun, by sharpshooter

From distant Artemisa, on the far side of the island, Ciro Redondo came to the Moncada one July 26. With him came a group of combatants, led by Fidel, to challenge the dictatorship on its own terrain: that of force. The people had lost their faith in peaceful solutions and were setting out on the long road of revolution that is now entering its final phase.

He was with [Fidel Castro] in his long days in the Isle of Pines prison and during the training period in Mexico. He arrived among the 82 on board the *Granma* as a soldier and was promoted directly to the rank of captain in our crude struggle that had its first anniversary five days after his death.

He was notable for his unshakable faith and his absolute fidelity to the revolution. He was a distinguished soldier among the most distinguished, always facing danger, always in the front line of the fighting, and it was here he was killed, leading his detachment, when he was only 26 years old.

On the eternal path of history, trodden only by the elect, goes Ciro Redondo, peerless friend, flawless revolutionary.

The eagle gaze of this people's captain must be captured as I recall it, in the bronze that will perpetuate the final victory. It is a way of doing him justice.

howcubanthe worldseemstous

withanunloadedgun,bysharpshooter

The voice of the distant world reaches the soil of our Sierra through the radio and newspapers, more explicit in describing events out there because it cannot relate the crimes that are committed here every day. Thus we learn about the disorder and deaths in Cyprus, Algeria, Ifni and Malaya. All of them have common features:

a) Government forces "have inflicted numerous casualties among the rebels";

b) There are no prisoners;

c) The government reports "nothing new";

d) All the revolutionaries, whatever the name of the country or region, are receiving "undercover aid from the communists."

How Cuban the world seems to us. It is the same thing everywhere. A group of patriots, armed or unarmed, rebels or not, is murdered and the armed oppressors chalk up points "after heavy fighting." All witnesses are killed, hence the absence of prisoners. The government never suffers casualties, and at times this is true since killing defenseless beings is not very dangerous. But there are also times when this is a tremendous lie and the S.M. [Sierra Maestra] can testify to this.

Finally, there is the hackneyed accusation they always trot out: "communists." Communists are people who turn to arms when they become tired of so much wretchedness, wherever it occurs in the world. "Democrats" are people who kill those who are angry about this, be they men, women or children.

The whole world is Cuban and what is happening here is happening everywhere: against brute force and injustice, the people will have the last word, the word that means victory.

This page: With Celia Sánchez.
Right: Sierra Maestra, Cuba, 1957.

thefirstcompatriot i'veseeninages...

(interviewbytheargentinejournalist, jorgericardomasetti,april1958)

When I woke up, I was disappointed. I had slept peacefully until 5 a.m. and had not heard any gunfire at all. The government troops had made a brief incursion but returned at once to their barracks on discovering that Che was not at La Otilia and that he was preparing an ambush.

I'd been eagerly awaiting the sound of gunfire, lying in the semi-darkness of the room, while Virelles, with the safety catch of his machine gun off, promised himself a trip to Buenos Aires just to hear some tangos. Around 2 a.m., Sorí Marín and I stretched out on the only two mattresses available. Placed together, they could have taken three people, but not the five I found when I woke up. Virelles had gone to take up his post while Cantellops snored in an armchair. Llibre appeared, scratching himself at the foot of the bed, and told me in distress how he had spent the whole night trying to break up a gathering of pimples that had unexpectedly appeared on his stomach.

In a few minutes, what had looked like a dormitory became a dining room, office and infirmary. Everyone was standing now and the only thing they were asking, whatever they were doing, was whether the *comandante* had arrived.

Guevara arrived at 6 a.m. While I watched admiringly as a group of lads busied themselves — doing something

I stopped doing a long time ago, washing their faces — groups of sweaty rebels loaded up with their light packs and heavy weapons began to come in from different directions. Their pockets were swollen with bullets and cartridge belts crossed chests without even the protection of buttonless shirts.

They were the people who had set out to ambush the troops of Sánchez Mosquera the previous night and were coming back weary, sleepy and still bursting with the desire to fight the troops of the detested colonel.

Shortly afterwards, Ernesto Guevara arrived. He was riding a mule, legs dangling, the curve of his back extended by the barrels of a Beretta and a rifle with telescopic lens, like two poles supporting the frame of his apparently big body.

As the mule approached I could see that, hanging from his waist, was a leather cartridge belt loaded with cartridges, and a pistol. From his shirt pockets two magazines protruded, while a camera hung from his neck and, from his chin, a few hairs that hoped to form a beard.

He calmly dismounted the mule, setting foot on the ground with his enormous muddy boots and as he came over to me, I calculated that he would be 178 centimeters tall. I noted that his asthma did not seem to inhibit him in any way.

Sorí Marín introduced us, watched by 20 soldiers who had never seen two Argentines together and who were somewhat let down to see that we greeted each other with a certain indifference.

The famous Che Guevara looked to me like a typical middle-class Argentine lad and also a rejuvenated caricature of Cantinflas.

He invited me to breakfast with him and we began to eat, almost in silence.

The first questions, logically, came from him. And, logically, they were about the political situation in Argentina.

My answers seemed to satisfy him, and not long after we started talking, we realized that we agreed on many things and that really, we were not two dangerous characters. Soon we were talking quite uninhibitedly, although with the slight reserve expected of two Argentines of the same generation, and we began to use the familiar *tú* form.

One of the peasant soldiers, who was trying to listen in, made some humorous comment to Guevara about how funny the Cubans found our way of talking. Our mutual amusement united us almost at once in a less reticent exchange.

Then I told him why I had traveled to the Sierra Maestra. The desire to clarify, especially for myself, what kind of revolution had been taking place in Cuba over the last 17 months; who was responsible; how was it possible to keep going for so long without the support of any foreign nation; why the Cuban people did not overthrow Batista once and for all if they were really with the revolutionaries; and dozens of other questions, many of which had already found answers after my journey to La Otilia:

after experiencing at close quarters the terror in the towns and the gunfire in the mountains; after seeing unarmed guerrillas participating in suicidal ambushes to get hold of some weapon with which they could really fight; after listening to illiterate peasants describing, each in his own voice, but all of them clearly, why they were fighting; after realizing that I was not in the midst of an army of fanatics that would accept anything from its leaders, but among a group of men who were aware that any deviation from the honest line they were so proud of would mean the end of everything and of the new rebellion.

But, in spite of everything, I was distrustful. I refused to let myself be totally carried away by my sympathies for the fighting peasants until I could submit to the severest scrutiny the ideas of the people who were leading them. I refused to admit once and for all that some Yankee consortium was not bending over backwards to support Fidel Castro, even though, on several occasions, planes that the U.S. aeronautical mission had handed over to Batista had fired on the places where I was.

My first specific question to Guevara, the young Argentine doctor turned hero *comandante* and creator of a revolution that had nothing to do with his own country, was:

"Why are you here?"

He had lit his pipe, and I my cigarette, and we settled in to a formal conversation that we knew would be long. He answered me in his calm way that the Cubans believe is characteristically Argentine, but that I would describe as a mixture of Cuban and Mexican.

"I am here simply because I believe that the only way to rid the Americas of dictators is to overthrow them — helping to bring about their fall in whatever way — the more direct the better."

"Are you not afraid that your intervention in the internal affairs of a country that is not your own might be seen as interference?"

"First of all, I consider that not only Argentina but all of Latin America is my country. My country's history is as glorious as that of Martí's, and it is in his land precisely that I abide by his doctrine. Besides, if I give myself, everything that I am, if I offer my blood for a cause that I consider just and popular, if I help a people to rid itself of a dictatorship that does indeed permit the interference of a foreign power that backs it with arms, with planes, with money and with military instructors, I cannot concede that my commitment should be described as interference. No country has yet denounced U.S. meddling in Cuban affairs and not a single newspaper has accused the Yankees of helping Batista to massacre his own people. But a lot of people are bothered about me. I am the interfering foreigner who is helping the rebels with his own flesh and blood. The people who supply arms for an internal war are not interfering. But I am!"

Guevara uses the pause to light his pipe, which has gone out. Everything he has said comes from what seem to be constantly smiling lips, without any stress on the words and in a totally impersonal manner. I, however, was totally serious. I knew that I had a lot of questions still to ask, but I already considered them absurd.

"And what about Fidel Castro's communism?"

Again the smile was clearly discernible. He took a long draw on his pipe and answered me in the same unconcerned tone as before.

"Fidel is not a communist. If he were, he'd at least have a few more weapons. But this revolution is exclusively Cuban. Or, better said, Latin American. Politically, Fidel and his movement might be described as 'revolutionary nationalist.' Of course he is anti-Yankee inasmuch as the Yankees are antirevolutionary. But, in fact, we are not brandishing some kind of proselytizing anti-Yankeeism. We are against the United States" — he stressed this to give perfect clarity to the concept — "because the United States is against our peoples."

I remained silent so that he would go on talking. It was horrifically hot and the warm smoke of the fresh tobacco was as invigorating as the coffee we were drinking from big glasses. Guevara's "S"-shaped pipe hung there smoking and swaying in harmony with the rhythms of his Cuban-Mexican chat as he continued.

"The main target of this communist nonsense is myself. Every single Yankee journalist who has come to the Sierra has begun by asking me about my activities in the Communist Party of Guatemala — taking it for granted that I was active in the communist party of that country — simply because I was and am a sincere admirer of the democratic government of Colonel Jacobo Arbenz."

"Did you occupy any position in that government?"

"No, never." He talks on calmly without taking his pipe from his mouth. "But when the U.S. invasion happened, I tried to get together a group of young men like myself, to fight the [United] fruit company mercenaries. In Guatemala it was necessary to fight and hardly anyone fought. It was necessary to resist and hardly anyone resisted."

I continued to listen to his account without asking further questions. There was no need.

"From there I escaped to Mexico, as the FBI agents had already begun to detain people, ensuring that all those who might represent a danger to the United Fruit government were killed at once. In the land of the Aztecs I once again met up with some of the July 26 people, whom I'd met in Guatemala, and became friendly with Raúl Castro, Fidel's younger brother.

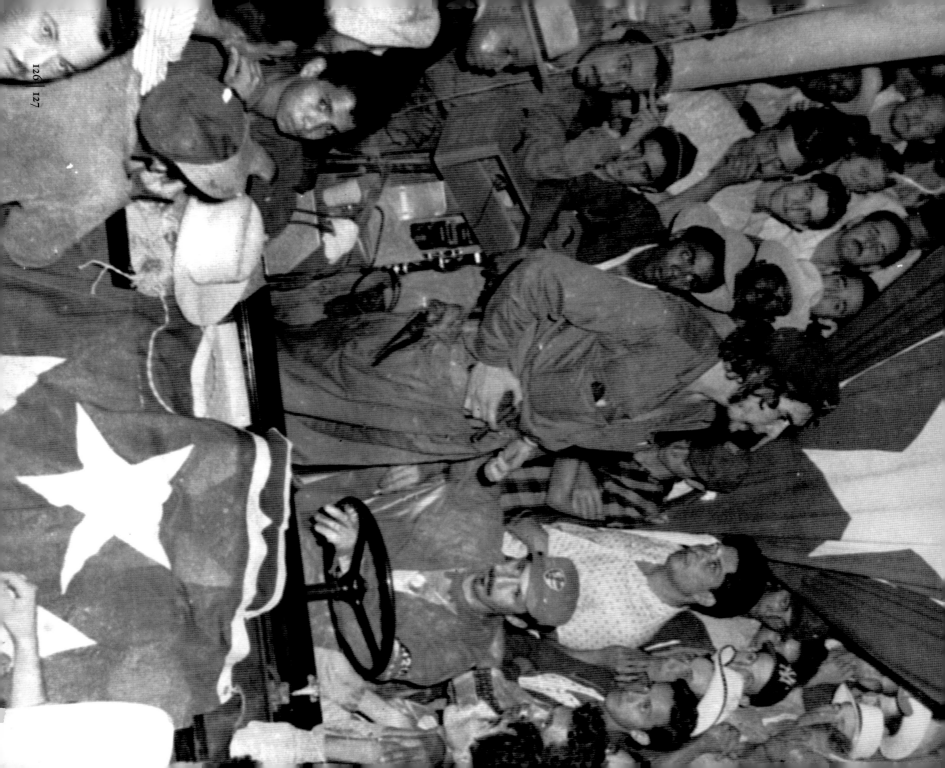

He introduced me to the leader of the movement when they had already begun to plan their invasion of Cuba."

Since his pipe had gone out again, he paused to light up a cigarette and offered me one. In order to show that I still existed behind the dense curtain of smoke, I asked him how he had come to join forces with the Cuban revolutionaries.

"I passed one whole night talking with Fidel. By dawn I was the doctor of his future expedition. In fact, after the experiences of my travels throughout Latin America and the finishing off of Guatemala, it didn't take much to persuade me to join any revolution against a dictator, but Fidel impressed me as an extraordinary man. He faced and resolved the most impossible situations. He had the extraordinary faith that, if he left for Cuba, he was going to arrive. That, once he arrived, he was going to fight. And that, in the fighting, he was going to win. I shared his optimism. It had to be done, we had to fight, to make it happen. To stop crying about it and to fight back. And to demonstrate to the people of his country that they could trust him, because he did what he said he would do, and he spoke his famous words: 'In '56 we will be free or we will be martyrs,' announcing that, before the year was out he was going to disembark somewhere in Cuba at the head of his expeditionary army,"

"And what happened with the disembarkation?"

The conversation was now the concern of more than 30 listeners. Sitting on the ground, with their weapons between their knees, their caps protecting their eyes from the reflections of the sun, "Che's men" smoked and listened attentively, without proffering a single word. A young, bearded doctor set and bandaged a finger perfectly, attending to nothing but what he was hearing. Libre, a passionate admirer of the leaders of the revolution but a vigilant doctrinarian, analyzed each of Che's words and scratched at the pimples on his stomach with nails discolored by the clayey earth. Virelles listened as he slept. Guillermito, a beardless youth with very long hair, cleaned his rifle with the same attention that the doctor gave to setting the finger. From somewhere, mingling with the smell of tobacco, wafted that of the pork they were frying in a pan in the open air.

Guevara went on with his account, with a cigarette in his mouth and his legs comfortably stretched out.

"When we arrived, they broke us up. We had an atrocious voyage in the yacht, the *Granma*, which took the 82 members of the expedition plus the crew. A storm threw us off course and most of us were suffering from seasickness. The water and food had run out and, to make matters worse, when we reached the island, the yacht became stranded in the mud. They were shooting at us without let up, from the air and the coast and, before long, only half of us were left alive, or half-alive if you consider the state we were in. All in all, out of the 82, only 12 of us were left with Fidel. And, at the beginning, our group was reduced to seven because the other five had scattered. This was all that was left of the invading army of the ambitious July 26 Movement. Lying there on the ground, without being able to fire for fear of giving ourselves away, we waited for Fidel's final decision, while we could hear the navy firing and the bursts of the air force machine guns in the distance."

Guevara let out a short laugh as he remembered.

"What a guy, this Fidel: you know, under cover of the noise of the machine guns he stood up and said to us, 'Listen how they're shooting at us. They're terrified. They're scared of us because they know we're going to get rid of them.' And, without another word, he picked up his gun and his pack and led our short column away. We were looking for Turquino, the highest and most inaccessible mountain in the Sierra, where we established our first camp. The peasants watched us go by without any show of friendliness. But Fidel didn't flinch. He greeted them with smiles and only took a few minutes to start up a more or less cordial conversation. When they refused to give us food, we continued our march without protest. It didn't take long for the peasants to realize that these bearded 'rebel' guys were exactly the opposite of the troops that were looking for us. While Batista's army laid their hands on everything they fancied in their huts — including the women, of course — Fidel Castro's people respected the peasants' property and paid generously for everything they consumed. We noted, not without surprise, that the peasants were disconcerted by our behavior. They were used to the treatment meted out by Batista's army. They were slowly becoming real friends and, as we accumulated encounters with groups of government troops in the mountains, many expressed their desire to join us. But these first arms began to bother the troops, and they marked the start of the most ferocious wave of terrorism imaginable.

"Every peasant was considered a potential rebel and was killed. If they found out that we had gone through a particular zone, they burned down the huts that we might have reached. If they came to any property and didn't find any men there because they were working or in the village, whether they imagined or not that they had joined our ranks, which were swelling every day, they shot everyone who remained at home. The terrorism practised by Batista's army was, without a doubt, our most effective ally at that time. It was the most brutally eloquent demonstration for the peasant communities that it was necessary to bring down the Batista regime."

The sound of a motor claimed the attention of us all.

"Plane!" some of them shouted and everyone ran inside La Otilia. In a matter of seconds, the animals' harnesses and the packs disappeared from the coffee drying floor, and nothing could be seen around the camp except the sun-whitened trees, the cement drying floor and the red clay track.

A dark gray plane appeared from behind the ridge and made two wide sweeps over La Otilia, quite high, but without firing a shot. Minutes later it disappeared.

We came out of the house as if we had been locked up for hours.

I reminded Guevara of my intention of meeting Fidel as soon as possible, to record my report and then return to the transmitter plant to try to get it directly to Buenos Aires. In a few minutes they found me a guide who knew the Jibacoa area, where Fidel was probably operating, and a more or less strong mule without too many sores.

"You'll have to leave now," Guevara told me, "to reach the first camp before it gets too late, and tomorrow morning you go on the Las Mercedes. They might be able to tell you there where to find Fidel. With luck, you'll locate him in three days."

I mounted the mule and said goodbye to them all, arranging to meet Guevara in La Mesa some days later when I would return with my recorded report. I gave Llibre several rolls of exposed film and two recorded tapes so that he could keep them for me in the transmitter plant.

It was about midday and the pork was frying again now that the plane scare was over. The smell of fat that at first made me so nauseous, now seemed delicious. The incredibly pure Sierra Maestra air was a great tonic for my stomach. Sorí Marín brought me half a dozen bananas that this time — and

I never understood why — were called *malteños*.

Guevara urged the guide to be very careful as we approached Las Minas.

"He's the first compatriot I've seen in ages," he shouted, laughing, "and I want him to survive at least until he can send the report to Buenos Aires."

"*Chau*," I called from the distance.

And about 30 voices answered, laughing and shouting, as if it were the funniest farewell they could imagine.

We branched off the path leading to La Otilia and crossed a coffee field. The beans were still green and gave off the pure aroma of fresh plants. While distracted — trying to peel *malteños* some 40 centimeters long — the branches sometimes tried to snatch my cap. But the proximity of Las Minas, though it didn't remove my appetite, captured my attention much more than the question of guiding the mule or peeling the bananas. My guide, who had a nickname more fitting for a leggy French showgirl than for a bearded and almost toothless peasant — "Nini" — was a few meters ahead, mounted on a small short-legged mule. Suddenly he dismounted and slid noiselessly toward me over the cushion of leaves. Before he got to me I had also dismounted and we moved away from the animals at once. The sound of branches hitting something like the steel helmet of a soldier could now be heard clearly. Nini released the safety catch of his pistol.

"Hey, *compay*!" he suddenly shouted. A peasant advanced with difficulty through the coffee trees trying, as much as he could, to prevent the branches from hitting the light rectangular box of white wood that he carried on his shoulder.

"What's news?" he replied, gasping for breath.

themurdered puppy.

Sierra Maestra, Cuba, 1957.

For all the harshness of conditions in the Sierra Maestra, the day was superb. We were hiking through Agua Revés, one of the steepest and most labyrinthine valleys in the Turquino basin, patiently following Sánchez Mosquera's troops. The relentless killer had left a trail of burned-out farms, sadness and despair throughout the entire region. But his trail led him, by necessity, to ascend along one of the two or three points of the Sierra where we knew Camilo [Cienfuegos] would be: either the

Nevada ridge, or the area we called the "Ridge of the Crippled," now known as the "Ridge of the Dead."

Camilo had left hurriedly with about a dozen men, part of his forward detachment, and this small number had to be divided up in three different places to stop a column of over a hundred soldiers. My mission was to attack Sánchez Mosquera from behind and surround him. Our fundamental aim was encirclement; we therefore followed him patiently, over a considerable distance, past the painful trail of burning peasant houses, set alight by the enemy's rearguard. The enemy troops were far away, but we could hear their shouts. We didn't know how many there were in all. Our column advanced with difficulty along the slopes, while the enemy advanced through the center of a narrow valley.

Everything would have been perfect had it not been for our new mascot, a little hunting dog only a few weeks old. Despite repeated attempts by Félix [Mendoza] to scare the animal back to our center of operations — a house where the cooks were staying — the puppy continued to trail behind the column. In that part of the Sierra Maestra it is extremely difficult to move along the slopes because there are no paths. We made it through a difficult pelúa, a spot where the "tomb" — old, dead trees — was covered by new growth, though the going was extremely laborious. We jumped over the trunks and thicket trying not to lose contact with our guides.

In these conditions the small column marched in silence, hardly a broken branch disturbing the usual murmurings of the mountain. But suddenly this code of silence was broken by the disconsolate, nervous barking of the pup. He was falling behind and was desperately barking for his owners to come and get him out of his trouble. Somebody went and picked up the little animal and we continued, but as we were resting in a creek bed with a lookout keeping an eye on enemy movements, the dog started up again with its hysterical howling. Comforting words no longer had any effect; the animal, afraid we would leave it behind, howled desperately.

I remember my emphatic order: "Félix, that dog must stop its howling once and for all. You're in charge; strangle it. There will be no more barking." Félix regarded me with eyes that said nothing. In the middle of our exhausted ranks, as if marking the center of a circle, stood Félix and the dog. Very slowly he took out a rope, placed it around the animal's neck, and began to pull. The affectionate movements of the dog's tail became suddenly convulsive, before gradually dying out, accompanied by a steady moan that escaped from its throat, despite the firm grip. I don't know how long it took for the end to come, but to all of us it seemed like forever. The puppy, after a last nervous shudder, stopped writhing. There it lay, sprawled out, its little head spread over the twigs.

We continued the march without even a word about the incident. Sánchez Mosquera's troops had gained some ground and shortly afterwards we heard gunfire. We quickly descended the slopes, amid the difficult terrain, searching for the best path to reach the rear guard. We knew that Camilo had attacked. It took us a considerable amount of time to reach the last house before starting up the other side, moving carefully because we imagined that we might come upon the enemy any moment. The exchange of fire had been intense, but it had not lasted long and we were all tense with expectation. The last house was abandoned. There was no sign of the troops. Two scouts climbed the "Ridge of the Crippled" and soon returned with the news: "There is a grave up above. We dug it up and found one of the metal-heads buried." They also brought the identity papers of the victim, found in his shirt pocket. There had been a clash and one man was killed. The dead man was theirs, but that was all we knew.

We returned slowly, discouraged. Two scouting parties came upon a large number of footprints along both sides of the ridge of the Maestra, but nothing else. We made the return trip slowly, this time through the valley.

We arrived during the night at a house, also vacant. It was the Mar Verde homestead where we could rest. Soon a pig was cooked along with some yucca, and we ate. Someone started to sing along to a guitar, since the peasant houses had been hastily abandoned with all their belongings still inside.

I don't know whether it was the sentimental tune, or the darkness of night, or just plain exhaustion. What happened, though, is that Félix, seated on the ground to eat, dropped a bone. One of the house dogs came up meekly and took it. Félix put his hand on its head, and the dog looked at him. Félix looked back at the dog, and then he and I exchanged a guilty look. We were suddenly silent.

An imperceptible stirring came over us. There, in our presence, with its mild, mischievous and slightly reproachful gaze, observing us through the eyes of another dog, was the murdered puppy.

...the measure of all things, speaks here through my mouth and narrates in my language that which my eyes have seen." This quote from Guevara's juvenilia — valid for all the years to come, all the years of his life — reminds us of the statement that the writer Pablo de la Torriente Brau made as he left for the Spanish Civil War: "...my eyes were made to see extraordinary things. And my typewriter to tell them. And that is all."

To that language — the written word — Che would add another: the photographic image. Che's relationship with photography was two-fold: as the subject of photography, today we find him in innumerable books and other publications, smiling or severe, in a beret or unkempt, always charismatic; as a photographer himself, we imagine him examining his equipment, holding the telephoto lens, traveling in some part of the world with his camera around his neck. Here in this intimate personal album is a fragment of the unknown story of Che the photographer as he looked at the world on our behalf.

...the mountain colors of the mountains, the young recruits of the Minas de Frío and a campesino protest in the first years of the Cuban Revolution. There follows an image of movement in a New Delhi street and an abstract vision of an industrial structure. In the canals of the Zapata Swamp, in Cuba, a small boat is pursued by the lens of the witness, looking down from a helicopter.

Finally, we see that same witness, looking at the camera, at his own camera, after a terrible, hazardous campaign in the Congo. Che photographed himself in the room in Tanzania where he had lived during that period, a photograph for which he had prepared his body and his spirit "with the delight of an artist."

An "artist of guerrilla warfare," as Fidel called him, Che was also an artist of words and photographs, which are engraved in our memories with tenacity and passion, beauty and sensitivity. The measure of all things. And that is all.

—VC

behind the lens

Above: Mexico, 1955.
Right: Mexico, 1955.

Above: Mexico, 1955.
Right: Mexico, 1955.

Both pages: Scaling Mt Popocatepetl, Mexico, 1955.

Above: Self-Portrait. Archeological ruins at Mitla, Mexico, 1954.
Right: Chac-Mool in the The Thousand Columns. Chichén-Itza, Mexico, 1955.

Above: The Castle. Chichén-Itza, Mexico, 1955.
Right: The Temple of the Warriors. Chichén-Itza, Mexico, 1955.

Above: Quadrangle of The Nuns. Uxmal, Mexico, 1955.
Right: Mar Verde, Sierra Maestra, Cuba, 1963.

Above: Mexico, 1955.
Right: Rally. Caney de las Mercedes, Cuba, 1959.
Following page: Profile of Fidel (right). Caney de las Mercedes, Cuba, 1959.

Left: Camilo Cienfuegos School Campus, Sierra Maestra, Cuba, 1959.

Right: Construction of the Camilo Cienfuegos School Campus, Sierra Maestra, Cuba, 1959.

Following page: Industrialization in progress. Oriente, Cuba, 1961.

Above: Construction of the José Martí housing project. Havana, Cuba, 1959.
Right: From a helicopter. Zapata Swamp, Cuba, 1959.

Above: Southeast Asia, 1959.
Below: India, 1959.

Above: India, 1959.
Below: India, 1959.

Left: Self-Portrait. Argentina, 1951.
Right: Self-Portrait. Cuba, 1959.
Following page: Self-Portrait. Tanzania, 1966.

he the witness: here, we present a brief montage of the interviews Che conducted, responding to questions put by journalists. In these interviews, we see his rapid answers to the curiosity, harassment or bad faith of his questioners, never neglecting to speak his mind or state shared truths and necessary criticisms.

In this participatory, sincere approach, Che does not flee from confrontation but faces it, offering his point of view. He does not avoid criticism, or self-criticism, but uses them as yet another weapon in the revolutionary struggle.

The images offered here reveal different aspects of his sometimes difficult role as interviewee. While we lack graphic evidence of his first interview, described in the diary of his travels through Argentina ("It was here that the first report about me was done for a Tucumán newspaper..."), we do have photographs of him facing the questions of a journalist in the middle of Cuba's

Sierra Maestra, or firing his ripostes into radio or television microphones. The caricaturists' pencils capture the story from a humorous point of view and trace the essential features of his personality, sometimes confirming the comment of his compatriot Jorge Ricardo Masetti, when he saw him for the first time in the Cuban mountains: he "looked to me like a... rejuvenated caricature of Cantinflas."

From the transcription of the interview given to Radio Rivadavia in Argentina a few months after the triumph of the revolution in Cuba, this sharp-witted interviewee reminds us of matters that are brutally relevant today:

If [the International Monetary Fund] is an element of liberation for Latin America, I believe that it should have demonstrated that. Until now, I have not been aware of any such demonstration. The IMF performs an entirely different function: precisely that of ensuring that capital based outside of Latin America controls all of Latin America.

the press with che

eduardo galeano

profile a revolutionary

On Wednesday night, Che Guevara responded to a thousand questions: swarming journalists fired them off mercilessly and Che had the opportunity to demonstrate his political ability. With no respite, he was made to leap from problems of economic development to Canada's admission into the OAS [Organization of American States]; from here, to Cuba's relations with the countries of the Eastern Bloc, and then to the issue of the Pan American airplane that had been hijacked [to Cuba] that very day. Furthermore, he also had to put up with impertinence and stupidity, which he turned to his advantage where necessary, taking the bull by the horns and wielding his irony at the cost of more than one journalist. One man with an English accent said, "I'm a British journalist. Are we or are we not at war?"

"That's not a very British question," replied Che.

Then, with visible indignation, he told Milton Fontaina of Saeta TV, "I do not have an ex-homeland. You should know, sir, that my country is much greater than yours: Latin America is my country." The applause resounded in the room of the Playa Hotel and many voices began to speak at once. "I'm not asking how many of you there are, but just that you keep coming," said Che, politely requesting that they put their questions one at a time.

"I was born in Argentina. But permit me to point out that Martí and Fidel are Latin Americans. My cultural substratum is Argentine but, at the same time, I feel as Cuban as anybody else. I feel the suffering of any country of the Americas and elsewhere in the world as well."

To lend a note of color to my article, I'd like to ask you how you work, if you drink, if you smoke and if you like women.

"I don't drink. I smoke. I would cease to be a man if I didn't like women. I would cease to be a revolutionary if, for that or any other reason, I did not fulfill my revolutionary duties to the full. I work 16 to 18 hours a day and sleep six hours a day when I can, if not less.

"I consider that I have a mission to accomplish in this world, for the sake of which I must sacrifice everything, everyday pleasures, a home, personal security and maybe my own life. This is my commitment and I can never be free of it as long as I live."

interviewwithjeandaniel

"Guevara, do you consider that Cuba could have done anything else but proclaim, in April 1961, its solemn and total adhesion of this Caribbean republic to Marxism-Leninism?"

Preparing to answer, Che becomes suddenly serious and abandons the charm Cubans use so freely.

"If you are asking me this question because we are in Algeria and because you wish to know if a revolution can be carried out by an underdeveloped country, in spite of imperialism, without becoming part of the sphere of communist nations, I'll tell you this: maybe; I don't know; it's possible. I have doubts, but it is not for me to judge.

"But if your question is to get an idea of the Cuban experience, then I can answer categorically: No, no we cannot do it any other way and, after a certain point, we did not wish to do it any other way. Our commitment to the Eastern Bloc is 50 percent the result of external pressure and 50 percent the result of a positive decision. In the situation in which we have found ourselves, that had given us a better idea than anything or anyone of what imperialism is, we have learned that, for us, it is the best way to fight effectively.

"It is also because of something else, to answer your rather too direct question. We deplore the disagreements within the communist family as they are occurring right at the time that we are joining this family,

"...In Cuba, we have been publishing from the outset Soviet and Chinese texts, with equal respect for both. If we have some role to play, it consists of contributing to the unity of the communist world. Perhaps we may manage to make ourselves heard and to mobilize effectively for this unity, by virtue of the fact of our particular geographic situation, and also because we can speak as victors over imperialism."

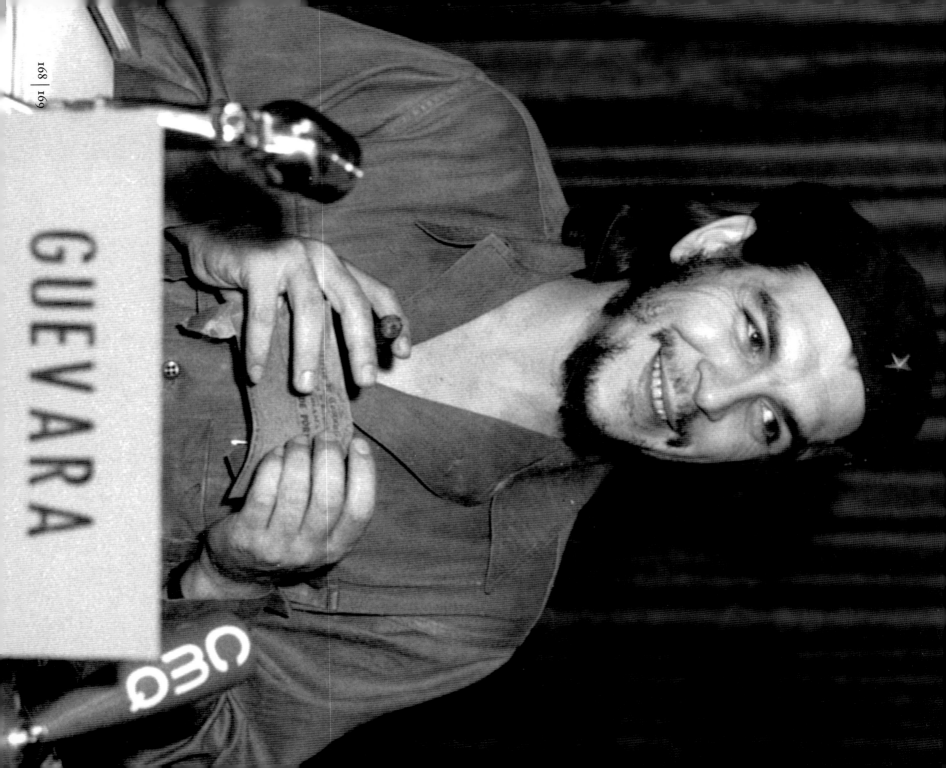

GUEVARA

a delicate word
(november 11, 1963)

There are several factors that account for the drop in [the economy's] profitability and quality. In what order would you put the following: bureaucratism, the blockade, lack of technical personnel, disorganization, union problems...?

"I would put the blockade first. I would say that you have presented these factors as though they were independent of each other, when they are the direct result of the blockade and aggression.

"For example, it is true that we lack technical capacity. A major part of the blame lies with those who have left the country to join the imperialist world, either out of cowardice or selfishness. This problem too, then, is caused by the blockade and aggression.

"I would put bureaucratism in second place, but bureaucratism is a delicate word."

interviewwith studentsfromthe unitedstates

After he had spoken at length with the students, they asked Che Guevara what he liked least about the revolution. The minister for industry responded:

"What I least like is our occasional lack of courage in confronting certain realities, sometimes economic and sometimes political, but especially economic. At times we have had

compañeros adopting the ostrich approach, burying their heads in the sand. We have blamed drought, imperialism... for our economic problems and, at times, when we have not wanted to broadcast the bad news, we have hesitated, and then only the [U.S.'s] Voice of America version has remained."

thegreatdifficultyisin upholdingstandards ofbehavior...

(interviewforradiorivadaviaofargentina,november3,1959)

In a report recorded in Havana and broadcast here tonight by Radio Rivadavia, Ernesto Che Guevara, commander of the Cuban Revolutionary Army, stated that, "few government leaders have been able to go to the United States and return with a clear conscience, as our Prime Minister Fidel Castro has done." [Fidel Castro went to the United States in April 1959].

Comandante Guevara made this statement about Fidel Castro in reference to the difference in conduct "one observes in movements before and after coming to power. Once one is in power," Guevara added, "the great difficulty is in upholding standards of behavior, in the face of the inevitable attacks by foreign monopoly capitalism and economic pressures.

"If these standards could be maintained in Latin America, enough political cohesion would be achieved to effectively defend its position in the international field, like the stance that has been adopted by the Afro-Asian countries in adhering to the so-called Bandung Pact [forerunner to the Nonaligned Movement]. Despite huge differences in their social systems, they have gone from practically socialist systems to international sultanates, sustaining a cohesion that is enviable for our countries of the Americas."

Referring to the International Monetary Fund (IMF), *Comandante* Guevara stated that, "If it is an element of liberation for Latin America, I believe that it should have demonstrated that. Until now, I have not been aware of any such demonstration. The IMF performs an entirely different function: precisely that of ensuring that capital based outside of Latin America controls all of Latin America."

Guevara said that the IMF "knows that in a case of aggression against us, we shall respond in the measure in which they know we do things. The interests of the IMF represent the big international interests that today seem to be established and concentrated in Wall Street."

"The complex problem of the deficit in the trade balance," he said, "can be resolved by diversifying production and diversifying foreign trade relations. My trip to the countries of Africa and Asia is in accordance with the decision of the Cuban Government to seek new markets all over the world. We aim to trade with countries everywhere — there are no ideological barriers in trade."

Guevara also said, "The only thing that can concern Cuba in foreign countries is what products they have to exchange for Cuban products and under what conditions they wish to do so."

He announced that during his foreign tour, and afterwards, he had signed or was about to sign trade agreements with a number of countries and that there were possibilities for Cuba to trade with Yugoslavia, India, Ceylon, Indonesia, Denmark and Pakistan.

He indicated that the countries he visited are in political-social circumstances similar to those of Cuba and that "they are fighting for their freedom, because their markets and foreign trade are controlled by colonial interests."

"They need," he added, "integral agrarian reform, and then they need to struggle to industrialize. Cuba is aligned with them in taking the same road toward a total recovery of the country."

He reiterated that Cuba is considering developing trade relations with the countries of Europe, both East and West, "since we believe that trade is one thing and ideological problems are quite another."

He noted that Cuba is interested in focusing on trade with other countries of the Americas, and that preference would be given to any negotiations undertaken with a Latin American country over those with countries of other continents.

After saying that economic definition leads directly to political definition, *Comandante* Guevara stated that, "the Cuban sectors opposing the present revolutionary government are capitalist parasites directly affected by the government's work, among them the big landowners."

He mentioned a large U.S.-controlled estate of 150,000 hectares — Atlántico del Golfo — noting that such interests are related to a certain type of U.S. landowning capital that "in some cases

have financed the coup attempts we have seen of late. We are in no doubt," he added, "that there will be more of them in future."

Referring to popular support for the revolutionary government of Cuba, Guevara said that it "comes from all sectors with something to gain in economic and moral terms: the peasants and workers, basically, and middle-class sectors, including all kinds of professionals and honest traders."

"People," he added, "are nothing but the representation of an ideology, a way of thinking, and this way of thinking must be sustained by a broad mass base. There are movements in Latin America that are able to create a nexus of solidarity and support for any position that means rejecting the economic and political subjugation of Latin America.

"General Cárdenas in Mexico, Larrazábal in Venezuela, Palacios in Argentina, De Aranha in Brazil, and others," he added, "meet these conditions to a greater or lesser degree."

Comandante Guevara indicated that "the structure of any Latin American movement that might have the same basic features, which would be so easy to attain among peoples with a similar economic structure and a similar political orientation with regard to what the masses desire, would be a very salutary measure in the development of Latin America's future struggle for her complete liberation."

He said, "the magnificent speech given by General Cárdenas in Havana on July 26 this year has contributed to consolidating relations between Cuba and the state of Mexico."

Finally, the *comandante* said, "the fact that there is not a single stalk of wheat in all of Cuba is one basis for discussions that could lead to a trade agreement being reached between Argentina and Cuba."

He clarified that he has not renounced his Argentine citizenship despite the fact that Cuban Government has bestowed upon him Cuban citizenship "from birth" and added that it is difficult for him to travel to the land where he was born, "because the intensity of the work carried out by members of the revolutionary government makes it practically impossible to leave the country unless it is for some particular goal, like, for example, our trip to the East."

friendship crosses the life of this man, from his childhood, when he played in the trenches built in the backyard of the house in Altagracia, reconstructing the daring deeds of the Spanish Civil War, to the final battle of the Quebrada del Yuro in October 1967.

This book is steeped in that beautiful, human emotion: in every chapter it is possible to underline a name or highlight an anecdote about friendship and its great worth. The adventurous journeys throughout Argentina or the Americas and the guerrilla experiences in two continents offer facts and stories where, from both light and shadow, friendship displays Ernesto's humanity and sense of awe.

But this is only a brief chapter, with the few lines which follow taken from here and there and written from, for and in favor of friendship.

This chapter, or even this entire book, could be dedicated to the great friendship of Che's life, a symbol of friendship itself: his friendship with Camilo Cienfuegos. The following words are taken from Che's prologue to *Guerrilla Warfare*: "...to its great captain, to the greatest guerrilla leader born in this revolution, to the flawless revolutionary and brother-in-arms."

The letter from Camilo which is included in this chapter, written in his labored calligraphy, is a part of the dialogue which these two men maintained through the din of combat and the complexities of human relationships in crucial moments of profound change. In a speech-homage to his *compañero* of the invasion, Che left us these wise, early words:

"*Revolutions are not absolutely pure movements; they are carried out by humans; brewed from internal battles, ambitions and mutual ignorance. All of this, once it is overcome, converts itself into a stage of history which, for better or worse, rightly or wrongly, becomes silent and disappears.*

"*Our story, too, is full of these disagreements, full of these battles which were sometimes of great violence, full of our self-ignorance... It is here that lay a great deal of work for Camilo, who does not yet know himself well. And this was evidently a unifying factor.*"

We have also included Che's memoir of El Patojo, an illustration of the friendship born of loneliness and the battle for survival in Mexico after the two left Guatemala in the aftermath of the 1954 military coup that overthrew the government of Jacobo Arbenz.

In the notes which recount that moment, Ernesto defines the trait common to the new friends: "His name is Julio Roberto Cáceres Valle, and he also seems under the sway of this obsession for traveling."

Together they "got to know all of Mexico City, walking from one end to another, delivering the atrocious photographs we had taken. We battled with all kinds of clients, trying to convince them that the little boy in the photo was really very cute and it was really a great bargain to pay a Mexican *peso* for such a marvel."

From Cuba, where he went to work following the triumph of the revolution in 1959, El Patojo left to fight for the independence of his homeland Guatemala; he fell in one of the combats of the nascent guerrilla army. The last tale of Che's *Episodes from the Revolutionary War* is also a farewell to this friend who was "an introvert, highly intelligent, broadly cultured, sensitive, [who] matured steadily and in his last moments was ready to put his great sensibilities at the service of his people."

The dialogue of friendship continues in this chapter with two texts which converse over time and distance. The first is a letter written in Mexico in October 1956, which Ernesto sent to his friend from university days, Tita Infante, "hidden and without horizons," but on the verge of defining his life's direction: "I'm only waiting to see what happens with the revolution; if it works out well, I'm heading for Cuba..." The other document is a moving testimony, written by Tita with whom he exchanged letters over many years. It is a souvenir of a love from his youth in Córdoba, written one year after the death of Che, whom she describes as "perhaps the most authentic of world citizens."

—VC

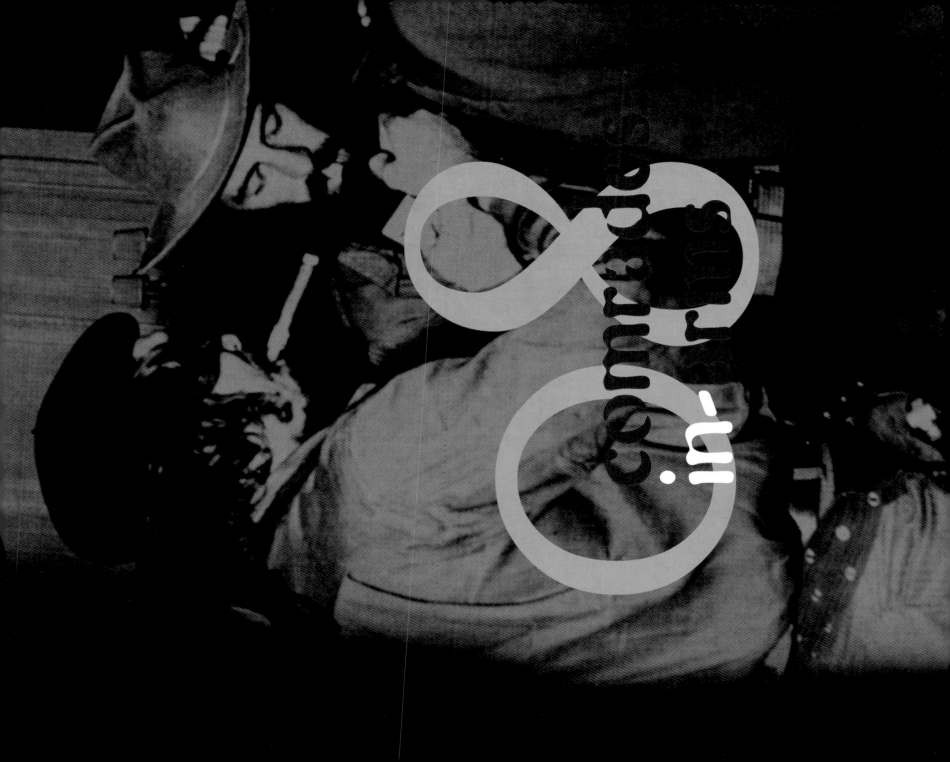

thegiantdoes well...totake careofyou...

(letterfromcamilocienfuegos)

April 24/58

Che, brother of my soul,

I received your note. I see that Fidel has put you at the head of the Military Academy, and I am very glad because that way we can count on a future of first-rate soldiers.

When they told me that you were coming to "give us the gift of your presence," I wasn't very pleased. You have undertaken the most important role in this conflict. If we needed you at this insurrectional stage, Cuba will need you more once the war is over; the Giant does well, therefore, to take care of you.

I would very much like to be always by your side. You were my leader for a long time, and you will continue to be that forever. Thanks to you I now have the chance to be more useful. I would do the unspeakable so you never look bad.

Your eternal sycophant,
Camilo

It was planned that this work would receive the approval of Camilo Cienfuegos, who was to have read and corrected it, when another destiny intervened. These lines and those that follow can be considered a homage from the Rebel Army to its great captain, the greatest guerrilla leader produced by this revolution, a flawless revolutionary and fraternal companion.

Camilo was the *compañero* of a hundred battles, the man trusted by Fidel in the difficult moments of the war, and the selfless fighter who always used sacrifice to temper his character and forge that of his troops. I believe that he would have approved of this manual synthesizing our experiences as guerrillas, the product of guerrilla life itself. It was he, however, who added to the framework of texts compiled here the essential vitality of his temperament, his intelligence and his audacity, to a degree which few of history's great personalities have achieved.

But Camilo should not be seen as an isolated hero accomplishing marvelous deeds through only the force of his genius. Instead, he should be considered an integral part of the people who made him, just as they make the heroes, martyrs and leaders of the battle's vast company, and under the same inflexible conditions.

I don't know if Camilo knew Danton's maxim for revolutionary movements: "audacity, audacity and more audacity." In any case, he practised it when in action, adding to it the spice of the other conditions necessary to the guerrilla: precise, rapid analysis of a situation and preemptive mediation for problems that would need future resolution.

Although these lines, a homage paid both personally and on behalf of an entire people to our hero, don't aim to act as a biography or even to relate his stories, Camilo was the subject of a thousand anecdotes; he created them naturally wherever he went. His ease among the people and his appreciation of them was integral to his personality. It is this which is sometimes unknown and forgotten, this which placed Camilo's distinctive stamp on all that belonged to him: the precious mark that so few men manage to leave as a result of their actions. Fidel has already said it: Camilo didn't have book learning, but he had the natural intelligence of the people. They had chosen him from among thousands to put him in his privileged position, which he attained through audacity, persistence, intelligence and devotion beyond compare.

Camilo practised loyalty as a religion. He was its devotee, shown as much in his personal loyalty towards Fidel, who embodies as no one else does the will of the people, as in his loyalty to the people themselves. The people and Fidel march united, and so marched the devotions of the ever-victorious guerrilla.

Who killed him?

It would be better to ask ourselves, "Who liquidated his physical being?", for the life of men such as Camilo finds its hereafter in the people. It does not end as long as the people do not authorize it.

The enemy killed him, it killed him because it wanted his death. There are no completely safe planes, pilots cannot gain all the necessary experience, and, overworked, he wanted to spend a few hours in Havana... his character killed him. Camilo didn't measure danger; he utilized it as a game, he played with it, he teased it, he courted it and he controlled it; with his guerrilla's mentality, a mere cloud could not detain or deviate him from the line he was following.

It happened at a time when an entire people knew, admired and loved him. It could have happened before and his story would have been the simple one of a guerrilla captain. There will be many Camilos, as Fidel has said. And there were other Camilos, I might add, whose lives ended before they could complete a magnificent cycle as he had done to enter into history.

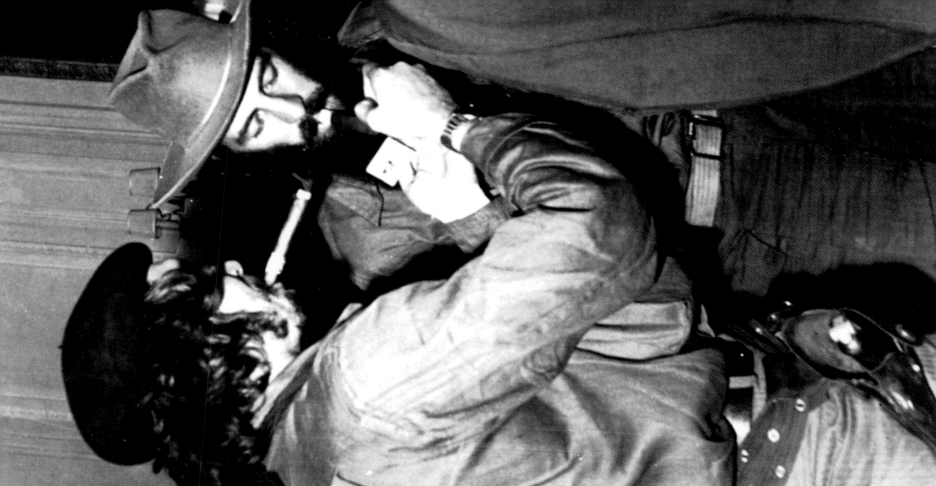

Camilo and those other Camilos (who did not make it and who will come) are the indication of the strength of the people. They are the highest expression of what a nation could manage to give, ready to go to war to defend their purest ideals and with their gaze fixed on the attainment of their most noble goals.

We aren't going to categorize him, to imprison him in molds: this would kill him. Let's leave him as we have done, in general outline, without adding precious touches to the socioeconomic ideology he hadn't perfectly defined. We emphasize that in this war of liberation there has not been a soldier comparable to Camilo. An exemplary revolutionary, a man of the people, an architect of this revolution that the Cuban nation has made its own, it was impossible that the slightest shadow of tiredness or disappointment could pass across his mind. Camilo, the guerrilla, is the subject of constant and daily evocation: he who did this or that, "one of Camilo's things," he who put his precise and indelible mark on the Cuban Revolution, he who is present in those who did not make it and those who are yet to come.

In his continuing and immortal renewal, Camilo is the image of the people.

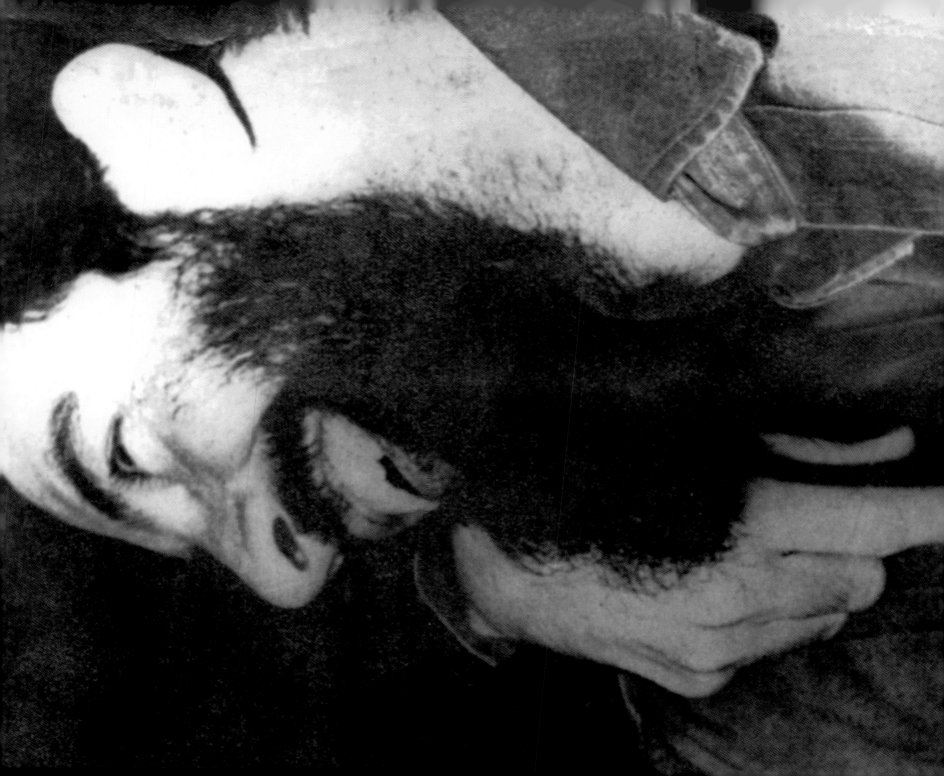

thisanarchicspirit thatleadsme todreamofhorizons

[circa October, 1956]

Dear Tita,

So much time has passed since I last wrote to you that I have lost the confidence born from our habitual communication. (I'm certain that you won't understand too much of my handwriting. I'll explain it all to you little by little.)

Firstly, my little Indian girl is now nine months old. She's quite sweet, full of life, etc.

Secondly and primarily: A while back some Cuban lads, revolutionaries, invited me to help the movement with my medical "knowledge," and I accepted, because you probably know that this is the kind of work which *me place*. I went to a ranch in the mountains to direct the training, vaccinate the troops, etc., but I had such bad luck (a Cubanism) that the police carted us all off, and since my papers were already dodgy (a Mexicanism) I had to swallow two months in jail, and the fact that they stole my typewriter as well as other bits and pieces (hence this handwritten missive). Afterwards the government committed the grave error of believing my word as a gentleman, and they freed me on the proviso that I would leave the country within 10 days. Three months later I'm still around, even though I'm hidden and without horizons in Mexico. I'm only waiting to see what happens with the revolution; if it works out well, I'm heading for Cuba; if it works out badly, I'll start to look for a country where I can set myself up. This year my life could change drastically, but it's already changed so many times that I don't get too surprised or moved by it.

Of course, all my scientific jobs fell through and now I am only an assiduous reader of little Karl [Marx] and little Friedrich [Engels] and all the other little ones. I forgot to tell you that when I was arrested they found several books of Russian and a card from the Mexican-Russian Exchange Institute, where I was studying the language because of this problem I have of conditioned reflexes.

It might interest you to know that my marriage is almost completely broken down, and will do so definitively next month. My wife is going to Peru to see her family, from whom she has been separated for eight years. There are certain bitter traces in the break up, as she was a loyal *compañera* and her revolutionary conduct was irreproachable during my enforced vacations. Our spiritual discordance was very great, however, and I live with this anarchic spirit that leads me to dream of horizons, since I have "the cross of your arms and the earth of your soul" as little Pablo [Neruda] said.

I'll sign off now. Don't write to me until after the next letter, which will have more news and a fixed address, at least.

An always affectionate hug from your friend,

Ernesto

thesunlessdayofbattle

(tributebytitainfanteoneyearafterche'sdeath)

When I was asked to collaborate in this Argentine testimony, I understood, and stated, that the undertaking was beyond me. But how could I deny such an honor? Or avoid such a duty!

Now, facing these still-blank pages, my goal seems unapproachable. To evoke the memory of a great man is always a difficult task. If, writing in 1968, that man is Ernesto Guevara, the task appears impossible.

A year has passed since my return to this country [Argentina] after a very long absence. The first newspapers that I read, my eyes startled, hands trembling, breath ragged, carried the slowly verified news of his tragic death: that unspeakable assassination for which the Americas will one day demand justification. One year, already so long ago. Still so fresh, like that blood drunk by the Bolivian soil, like that big-eyed gaze which transcends death, going beyond the bounds of time and space. His brave body on a miserable canvas mat, his beautiful head with the aureola of the guerrilla's beard and mane, his face that of Christ without the rictus of pain... Earth and wood, spring water, wild vitality... Ernesto has died, but he had already been born into eternity. He always lived joyously following the path to tragedy. Death ended his journey, but opened the doors to the life he had so desired. The memory of Ernesto, his life, his struggle, will always live on in the hearts of the peoples of this world: Ernesto Guevara was one of those men who was one of destiny's rare gifts to humanity.

One year on from his death, much has been written about Ernesto: books, articles, studies, essays, biographies. What can I say?

A close friendship united us over many years. For nearly six years we were in personal contact, and afterwards we communicated by letter. Our friendship began in 1947. In an anatomy amphitheater in the Faculty of Medicine, I often heard a warm, grave voice. The irony of this voice gave courage to both its owner and its listeners, as we future physicians faced a spectacle that shook even the most insensitive among us. By his accent, he, too, was from the provinces; from his appearance, a young man, handsome and self-assured... The fire which was to consume Ernesto's existence lay beneath his tender, wooden courtesy; but it already sparked in his gaze. A mix of shyness and haughtiness, perhaps even audacity, covered his profound intelligence and an insatiable desire to understand; there, deep below, lay an infinite capacity for love.

We never belonged to any of the same groups, either cultural or political; nor did we have the same circle of friends. Both of us, for different reasons, were a little unusual in that faculty. For Ernesto, it was perhaps because he knew that he would find very little of what he sought there. Our contact was therefore always on an individual basis, at the university, in cafés, at my house, infrequently at his... We also met in the Museum of Natural Sciences, where we used to meet every Wednesday "to study the phylogeny of the nervous system." At that time, we dedicated ourselves to studying fish, alternating between dissections, preparations, paraffin, microtomes, mounting cross-sections, microscope work, etc., sometimes with the assistance of an old German professor. But Ernesto's pleasant conversation shortened just a little those hours which were otherwise too long. He never missed an appointment, and he was always punctual. Never did he miss a call. What a strange bohemian he was!

Every time a decision turned out well, we would repeat the verses from Gutiérrez which we both loved:

**Don't shout slogans of victory
On the sunless day of battle.**

I often wondered afterwards how often Ernesto would have repeated these words, in the Sierra Maestra, in the Congo, in Bolivia... His entire life was a struggle, and it is perhaps for that reason that those verses so clearly belonged to him.

Many times I saw Ernesto worried, grave or pensive, yet never truly sad or bitter. I can't remember a single encounter which lacked his smile or that warm tenderness so appreciated by those who knew him well. In his conversation there was no room for the contemptible; he would be deeply critical in a brief phrase, and immediately follow it with something positive, moving on to a constructive future. Ernesto could not be perceived as being against something, but rather always for something. Perhaps because of this, he never suffered the slightest trace of malice.

Since Ernesto made the most of every minute, even on the bus, he generally appeared with a book in hand. Sometimes it was a volume of Freud: "I want to reread a clinical history for a case I'm interested in"; at other times a text book or a classic.

He never had extra money; quite the opposite. At that time he earned a living working with Dr. Pisani, doing research into allergies. His economic limitations, however, were never a particular worry for him, nor did they ever stop him from carrying out what

he saw as an obligation. Neither his apparent freedom from cares nor the lack of attention to his dress managed to hide his sober distinction.

A banal memory comes to mind... We often exchanged books, and I once lent Ernesto *El pescador de esponjas* (The Sponge Fisherman), by Panait Istrati. He really liked it, and we discussed it together. Rereading my copy, he had lost it, and had been waiting to buy another to replace it for me. Finally, he came across another copy of the same book. Yet mine was only the most modest little volume, badly bound, and bought in a second-hand bookshop in Avenida Corrientes!

We were united by a great trust and a deep level of intimacy, which allowed us to confide both the happy and shameful incidents of our personal lives. However, that modesty which characterized him meant that we could tell each other a lot without the need to speak too much.

While a student, Ernesto didn't work a lot but he did work effectively. Deep down in that young man, always ready for "adventure," feeling "the ribs of Rocinante beneath his heels" urging him to leave, there was a great thirst for knowledge. He did not seek to amass treasures in a complex mind, but rather he sought tirelessly for truth, and with truth his destiny. Everything about Ernesto was coherent, and every experience or fact, no matter what kind, was integrated into his being.

Ernesto graduated in less than six years, in spite of his travels, work, sport (at that time, rugby and golf) and the great part of his life that he dedicated to reading and cultivating friendships. Ernesto knew how to study; he went to the heart of a problem, and from there he stretched himself out as far as his plans allowed. He could stop and analyze at great depth when a problem impassioned him: leprology, allergies, neurophysiology, psychology... By the same token, the night before an exam Ernesto could ask over the phone for the classification of plants into A, B and C, according to the percentage of calories or protein they had... He skipped practicals and theory classes with the same ease as he leapt over obstacles. When he gave his word, however, he honored his promises at any cost: I saw him complete his Nutrition practicals after having passed the final exam.

Ernesto cultivated friendships with dedication and care, fed by his deep sense of humanity. For him, friendship imposed sacred duties and authorized rights of the same proportions; he practised both. He asked with the same naturalness as he gave, in all spheres of life.

Distance did not mean absence for Ernesto. In every journey, his more or less regular letters (according to the whims of the road or his financial state) continued the dialogue of friendship. A lover of photography, he sometimes sent images of the most varied circumstances of his life: sick in hospital in the south [of Argentina], unrecognizable in his skinniness; sitting on a wheel amid the indigenous people of the Brazilian jungle; fatter after a few weeks of rest, or in an advertisement from *Gráfico*. He kept the letters of his friends, and never let any go without a reply.

On his return from his second-last journey as a young man, Ernesto recalled the 20 days spent in Miami as the most difficult and bitter of his life, and not only because of the economic conditions he was forced to live in! (I won't go into detail, as the period is covered in all his biographies.)

While he was preparing for his last youthful journey, Ernesto came to my house to tell me a story. He recounted, with much laughter and a little annoyance, how the Venezuelan consul, who refused to give him a visa (in his last stay there, Ernesto had doubtless left a "bad memory" with the governors of Our America), had confused his asthma attack with a threatening case of cholera.

Until the day when we said our farewells, at a meeting in Ernesto's house of his closest friends, I only noted his great sobriety: he didn't smoke, he didn't drink either alcohol or coffee, and his diet was very strict. His asthma imposed living conditions on him which he maintained with perfect discipline.

Every letter from Ernesto was a literary page, full of affection, grace and irony. He retold his adventures and misadventures with brushstrokes of humor which removed the gravity even from the most difficult moments. In every country Ernesto immersed himself in what was most local and authentic, and his interests led him from Incan ruins to leper colonies and mines of copper and tungsten. He quickly became part of the life of the people, and found a place for himself in the social and political spheres. His stories were agreeable, with prose that was simple, yet pure and elegant. He painted objects and people with realism and objectivity, yet without euphemisms. When Ernesto spoke of his personal life, either with happiness or sadness, he did so with modesty and always asked for the complete discretion of his listener.

I think that even in the worst moments of his life, Ernesto's love of life was so great that he found optimism from his own internal logic: "When things are going badly, it consoles me to think that they could be going worse, and in any case, they could get better."

In August 1958, when I was preparing to leave Argentina, a young journalist I didn't know called me to arrange a meeting in a café: it was Masetti. He had just spent two months in the Sierra Maestra, and brought one letter for Ernesto's mother and one for me. He brought the special request that

we write as soon as we could; I still remember Ernesto's pseudonym, Teté Calvache, and various addresses in Havana. His affectionate nature, far from becoming hardened in the struggle, became richer, and he thought of his homeland, his mother and his friends with nostalgia. Masetti spoke at length of the Sierra Maestra, of everything and everyone: Fidel, Raúl, the camps... But nothing, for him, had the stature that Ernesto did, for his human characteristics, his bravery, his multifaceted capacities. If a civil registry, or a school, or bread-making, or the repair and manufacture of weapons had to be organized, there was Ernesto to take it on and run it. And in battle, he was always the first.

His legendary bravery was already being spoken about, and a collection of anecdotes was slowly taking form with the comments of the young Guatemalans who knew him, and who after the fall of Arbenz found a very peculiar refuge in Argentina.

I first heard of the victory [of the Cuban Revolution] in Florence on January 2.

So from that date, January 2, 1959, the life of Ernesto left the personal sphere and now belongs to history. There is nothing more I can add.

I therefore had the strange privilege of knowing him deeply, of having had his trust and sharing a great friendship which knew nothing of carelessness or

reticence. I met him when he was very young, when he was only Ernesto. But the future Ernesto Che Guevara was already in him at that time. From the years of his youth, I always saw Ernesto progress in his personal journey, ever moving forward, never stopping. Those who knew Ernesto well understood not only that "he did not stop until he reached the poles" but that he was going onward to his destiny, a destiny that was never one for a common life. I did not know how or when, but I was always certain that after a long journey he would arrive at that destiny; I was always surprised by the letter, the call, the article in the news, but I was never truly astonished.

Today, more than a year after his death, it is still difficult for me to order the countless memories and images in my memory and mind; they are so tinged with affection, so intermingled with pain and admiration.

Difficult to feel so close and yet so far away from his giant's figure, that demigod who recalls Greek legend and medieval heroes.

Difficult to unite such grandeur with his sensitivity and tenderness, his human richness.

Too warm to sculpt him from stone.

Too great to imagine him ours.

Ernesto Guevara, as Argentine as the greatest, was perhaps the most authentic of world citizens.

el patojo

A few days ago a cable brought the news of the death of some Guatemalan patriots, among them Julio Roberto Cáceres Valle.

In this difficult profession of a revolutionary, in the midst of class wars that are convulsing the entire continent, death is a frequent accident. But the death of a friend, a comrade during difficult hours and a sharer in dreams of better times, is always painful for the person who receives the news, and Julio Roberto was a great friend. He was short and frail; for that reason we called him "El Patojo," Guatemalan slang meaning "Shorty" or "Kid."

El Patojo had witnessed the birth of our revolution while in Mexico and had volunteered to join us. Fidel, however, did not want to bring any more foreigners into that struggle for national liberation in which I had the honor to participate.

A few days after the revolution triumphed, El Patojo sold his few belongings and, with only a small suitcase, appeared in Cuba. He worked in various branches of public administration, and he was the first head of personnel of the Department of Industrialization of INRA [National Institute of Agrarian Reform]. But he was never happy with his work. El Patojo was looking for something different; he was seeking the liberation of his own country. The revolution had changed him profoundly, as it had all of us. The bewildered young man who had left Guatemala without fully understanding the defeat had now become the fully conscious revolutionary.

The first time we met we were on a train, fleeing Guatemala, a couple of months after the [1954] fall of Arbenz. We were going to Tapachula, from where we could reach Mexico City. El Patojo was several years younger than I, but we immediately formed a lasting friendship. Together we made the trip from Chiapas to Mexico City; together we faced the same problems — we were both penniless, defeated and forced to earn a living in an indifferent if not hostile environment. El Patojo had no money and I only a few pesos; I bought a camera and, together, we undertook the illegal job of taking pictures of people in the city parks. Our partner was a Mexican who had a small darkroom where we developed the film. We got to know all of Mexico City, walking from one end to another, delivering the atrocious photographs we had taken. We battled with all kinds of clients, trying to convince them that the little boy in the photo was really very cute and it was really a great bargain to pay a Mexican peso for such a marvel. This is how we ate for several months. Little by little the contingencies of revolutionary life separated us. I have already said that Fidel did not want to bring him to Cuba, not because of any shortcomings of his, but to avoid turning our army into a mosaic of nationalities.

El Patojo had been a journalist, had studied physics at the University of Mexico, had left his studies and then returned to them, without ever getting very far. He earned his living in various places, at various jobs, and never asked for anything. I still do not know whether that sensitive and serious boy was overly timid, or too proud to recognize his weaknesses and his personal problems to approach a friend for help. El Patojo was an introvert, highly intelligent, broadly cultured, sensitive. He matured steadily and in his last moments was ready to put his great sensibilities at the service of his people. He belonged to the Partido Guatemalteco de Trabajo [Guatemalan Labor Party] and had disciplined himself in that life — he was developing into a fine revolutionary cadre. By then, little remained of his earlier hypersensitivity. Revolution purifies people, improves and develops them, just as the experienced farmer corrects the deficiencies of their crops and strengthens their good qualities.

After he came to Cuba we almost always lived in the same house, as was fitting for two old friends. But we no longer maintained our earlier intimacy in this new life, and I only suspected El Patojo's intentions when I sometimes saw him earnestly studying one of the native Indian languages of his country. One day he told me he was leaving, that the time had come for him to do his duty.

El Patojo had had no military training; he simply felt that duty called him. He was going to his country to fight, gun in hand, to somehow reproduce our guerrilla struggle. It was then that we had one of our few long talks. I limited myself to recommending strongly these three things: constant movement, constant wariness and eternal vigilance. Movement — never stay put; never spend two nights in the same place; never stop moving from one place to another. Wariness —

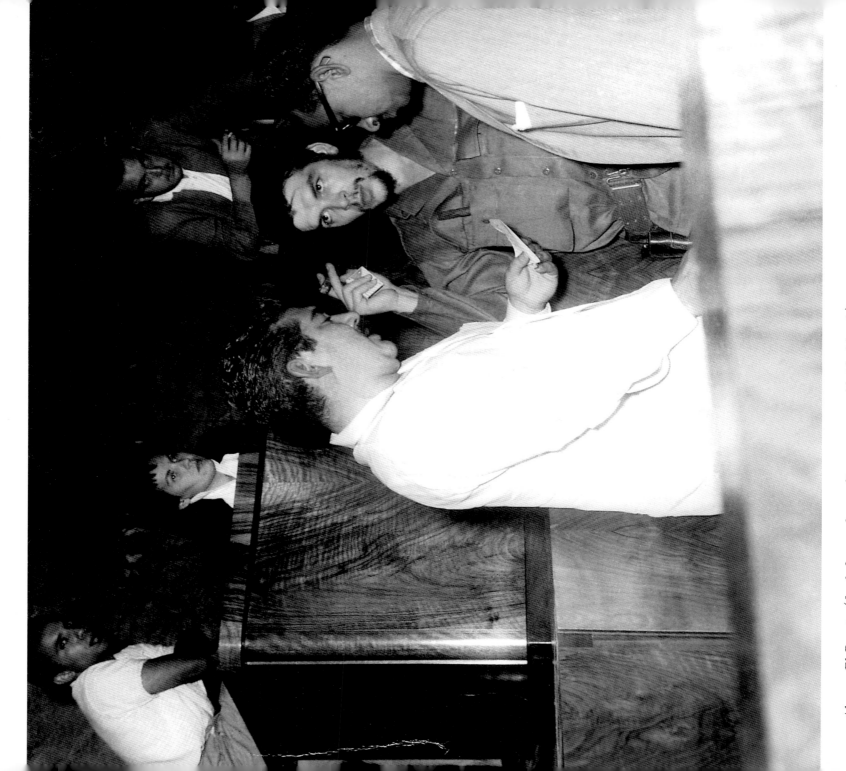

Above: El Patojo (far left, on the podium, next to Aleida March).

at the beginning, be wary even of your own shadow, friendly peasants, informants, guides, contacts; mistrust everything until you hold a liberated zone. Vigilance — constant guard duty; constant reconnaissance; establishment of a camp in a safe place and, above all, never sleep beneath a roof, never sleep in a house where you can be surrounded. This was the synthesis of our guerrilla experience; it was the only thing — along with a warm handshake — which I could give to my friend. Could I advise him not to do it? With what right? We had undertaken something at a time when it was believed impossible, and now he saw that it had succeeded.

El Patojo left and in time came the news of his death. At first we hoped there had been a confusion of names, that there had been some mistake, but unfortunately his body had been identified by his own mother; there could be no doubt he was dead. And not only he, but a group of comrades with him, all of them as brave, as selfless, as intelligent perhaps as he, but not known to us personally.

Once more there is the bitter taste of defeat and the unanswered question: Why did he not learn from the experience of others? Why did those men not heed more carefully the simple advice which we had given them? There is an urgent investigation into how it came about, how El Patojo died. We still do not know exactly what happened, but we do know that the region was poorly chosen, that the men were not physically prepared, that they were not sufficiently wary and, of course, that they were not sufficiently vigilant. The repressive army took them by surprise, killed a few, dispersed the rest, then returned to pursue them, and virtually annihilated them. They took some prisoners; others, like El Patojo, died in battle. After being dispersed, the

guerrillas were probably hunted down, as we had been after Alegría de Pío.

Once again youthful blood has fertilized the fields of the Americas to make freedom possible. Another battle has been lost; we must make time to weep for our fallen comrades while we sharpen our machetes. From the valuable and tragic experience of the cherished dead, we must firmly resolve not to repeat their errors, to avenge the death of each one of them with many victories, and to achieve definitive liberation.

When El Patojo left Cuba, he left nothing behind, nor did he leave any messages or personal belongings to worry about. Old mutual friends in Mexico, however, brought me some poems he had written and left there in a notebook. They are the last verses of a revolutionary; they are, in addition, a love song to the revolution, to the homeland and to a woman. To that woman whom El Patojo knew and loved in Cuba are addressed these final verses, this injunction:

Take this, it is only my heart
Hold it in your hand
And when the dawn arrives,
Open your hand
And let the sun warm it...

El Patojo's heart has remained among us, in the hands of his beloved and in the loving hands of an entire people, waiting to be warmed beneath the sun of a new day which will surely dawn for Guatemala and for all the Americas. Today, in the Ministry of Industry where he left many friends, there is a small school of statistics named "Julio Roberto Cáceres Valle" in his memory. Later, when Guatemala is free, his beloved name will surely be given to a school, a factory, a hospital, to any place where people fight and work to build a new society.

orking in the various roles he successively assumed after 1959, Che dedicated time and attention to responding to the bountiful correspondence he received. This tiny sample of *letters of candor* belongs to that other form of testimonial communication, his personal letters: here we have a handful of texts which show the author's opinions on the need for honesty and ethics, his defense of historical truth and his relationship with the Cuban press. To the media, Che sent two of the letters included here; in one of these cases, the request was made that the letter be published as his way of "letting off steam."

Including Che's epistolary texts in this book, it is impossible not to recall the crystalline definition which Pablo de la Torriente Brau sent from his exile in New York in 1936 to his comrades-in-arms, and the comrades of his dreams:

"My letters are the official record of my thoughts; I am not afraid to write what I think, with regard to either present or future, for my thought is not double-edged and it does not express double meanings. It is enough that they have one sharp, unequivocal blade, which offers them the firm, internal conviction of my acts."

That ethical resonance can be found in the letter Che sent to the Writers' and Artists' Union of Cuba (UNEAC), rejecting their complacent and

inaccurate description of his social origins as it appeared in the biographical note to *Episodes from the Revolutionary War*.

The long, handwritten letter addressed to Armando Hart ("My dear secretary" of the Communist Party at that time, responsible for its ideological work), included the outline of "a few small ideas on the culture of our vanguard and our people in general." Before proposing a program of political studies which would appeal to intelligence and creativity of thought, Che described the weaknesses he had discovered in this terrain:

"In this long vacation period I have had my nose buried in philosophy, something I have wanted to do for some time. I came across the first problem: nothing is published in Cuba, if we exclude the Soviet bricks which have the drawback of not letting you think, because the party has already done it for you and you just have to digest it. It's method is anti-Marxist as can be and, moreover, the books tend to be very bad."

The letter to Haydée Santamaría ("Dear Yeyé") is another homage to the friendships he forged during the revolutionary struggle, in which poetry and tenderness are not absent, as can be seen in one image Che evoked: though Haydée had become "a woman of letters with the power of creation... the way I like you best is on that day early in the new year, with all your fuses blown and firing volleys for miles around."

This diversity of approach in his letters, above all, reveals one common characteristic: for Che, epistolary communication was an important instrument throughout the different stages of his life. The wonderful thing, in his case, is to be able to follow the development of his letter writing capacity through countries, periods and situations, as this book attempts to do.

In the letters, one feels on many occasions the warmth of admiration and friendship. The way in which they were written, their content and spirit, also offers an insight into the anti-bureaucratic style and intent of the writer. His letter to Cuban Foreign Minister Raúl Roa was sent from a Cuban embassy in a French colony in Africa and the author types it directly on an unfamiliar typewriter, as the facsimile that has been preserved reveals.

Raúl Roa's reply to Che is included in this book as a tribute to their exchange of humor from two very different esthetic standpoints. This letter refers to the new situation of its recipient as an author of books, achieved with the publication of *Guerrilla Warfare*. Roa offers to "make use of his good standing with Mao so that 600 million copies can be published in the language of Lao-Tse." Letters from afar and of great candor.

—VC

to pablo
díaz gonzález

Havana, October 28, 1963
"Year of Organization"

Co. Pablo Díaz González, Administrator

Campo de Perf. Extr. de la Cuenca Central

Apartado 9. Majagua

Camagüey

Pablo,

I read your article. I must thank you for how well you portray me — too well,
I think. It seems that you also portray yourself quite well.

The first thing a revolutionary who writes history must do is to stick to the
truth like a finger in a glove. You may have done that but the glove is a boxing
glove and that doesn't count.

My advice: reread the article, take out everything you know to be untrue and
be careful with everything you are not certain is true.

Revolutionary greetings,

"Patria o Muerte. Venceremos."

Comandante Ernesto Che Guevara

to valentina gonzález bravo

Miss Valentina González Bravo
Narciso López Nº 35,
Morón, Camagüey

Dear Miss González,

I have read your letter in which you ask me to help you to acquire orthodox indoctrination in the events of "July 26."

I admire your interest in doing so and congratulate you for the efforts you are making and for the goals that inspire you.

I do not think that it is possible to write under the influence of orthodox indoctrination and, besides, there is no official version of July 26. I believe that writing is a way of facing up to concrete problems, a position one adopts toward life because of one's sensitivity.

Keep working so that triumph will crown your efforts. Overcoming adversities in the profession you have chosen is one of the best ways to improve.

With kind regards,

Dr. Ernesto Che Guevara,
Commander-in-Chief
La Cabaña Military Region

to Carlos franqui

Compañero **Carlos Franqui**
Director, *Revolución*
Havana

Compañero Franqui,

I didn't like the photo supplement published the other day: permit me to tell you this in total frankness, and to explain why, hoping that these lines will be published as a way of my "letting off steam."

Leaving aside petty details that do not speak well of the seriousness of the newspaper, such as those photos of soldiers aiming at a supposed enemy but with their eyes turned to the camera, there are a number of fundamental errors:

1) That diary extract is not entirely authentic. It was like Ilús. they asked me (during the war) if I had kept a diary of the invasion. I had, but in the form of very bare notes, for my personal use and, at the time, I had no opportunity to write them up. This was then done (I do not recall now what the circumstances were) by a gentleman from Santa Clara who turned out to be a bit of a "pedant" and who wanted to inflate the exploits by means of adjectives.

The small value that these few notes might have is destroyed when they lose their authenticity.

2) It is false that, for me, the war took second priority to attending the peasants. At the time, winning the war was the main thing and I believe that I gave everything I had to that end. After entering the Escambray Mountains, I gave two days' rest to troops who had been on the march for 45 days in extremely difficult conditions, and then I renewed our operations and we took Güinía de Miranda. If I sinned in any way, it was the opposite: too little attention to the difficult task of dealing with all the "cattle rustlers" who had taken up arms in those cursed foothills. Gutiérrez Menoyo and his gang vexed me no end, something I had to swallow in order to concern myself with the main task: The War.

3) It is false that Ramiro Valdés was a "close collaborator of Che in organizational matters" and I don't know how you, as editor, and knowing him so well, let this pass.

Ramirito was in the Moncada assault, prisoner on the Isle de Pines, he came on the *Gramma* as a lieutenant, rose to the rank of captain when I was named commander, he led a column as commander, was number two in the invasion and then led operations in the eastern region while I went to Santa Clara.

I consider that historical truth must be respected; capricious invention cannot lead to anything good. Therefore — and because I was an actor in this part of the drama — I write these critical lines in the hope that they may be constructive. I think that if you had revised the text the errors could have been avoided.

I wish you a happy Easter and a year to come without too many shocking headlines (because of what they bring),

Che

to Juan Ángel
cardi

Havana, November 11, 1963
"Year of Organization"

Compañero Juan Ángel Cardi,
Calle 17 N° 54 Apto 22
Vedado, Havana

Compañero,

I acknowledge receipt of your communication dated last October 3, in which you enclosed chapters from nine of your unpublished novels.

I have no objection to your using whatever you feel is appropriate from the Las Villas diary. Remember, however, that when it was published, it was embellished by the florid language of an ass-licker.

I read the chapter of *Pléyade* like someone examining a photograph of a familiar place but not finding it. It gives the impression that you have never been in the Sierra, and have not even spoken with the people who were there at the time. If you would permit me, I should like to tell you in a fraternal spirit that you have not captured the grandeur of the time in all its depth.

I'm noting this as an impression, not as literary criticism; simply as someone who is looking for a likeness in an old photo — a souvenir of a group of friends, for example — but who finds that some technical defect, or time itself, has rendered the subjects of the photo unrecognizable.

If this observation is of any use to you, I am gratified, if not, please do not be offended by my frankness. I don't know how old you are, nor your vocation as a writer. The only passion that guides me in this field of yours is conveying the truth (and do not take me here for a hard-line defender of socialist realism). I look at everything from this point of view.

My greetings and wishes for your success in your literary odyssey.

Comandante Ernesto Che Guevara

tobernabé
ordaz

May 26, 1964
"Year of the Economy"

Dr. Eduardo B. Ordaz Ducungé
Director, Psychiatric Hospital
Havana

Dear Ordaz,

Thank you for the journal. Although I have very little time, the material seems very interesting and I shall try to have a look at it.

I'm curious about something else. How can 6,300 copies of a specialist review be printed when there are not even that many doctors in Cuba?

Something keeps gnawing away at my mind and is driving my spirit to the verge of a neuro-economic psychosis. Are the rats using the journal to improve their psychiatric knowledge or to satisfy their stomachs? Or maybe each patient has a copy by their bed?

In any case, there are 3,000 copies too many in the print-run and I urge you to give this some thought. Seriously, though, the journal is good, but the print run is intolerable. Believe me, because madmen always tell the truth.

Yours in the revolution,
"Patria o Muerte. Venceremos."
Comandante Ernesto Che Guevara

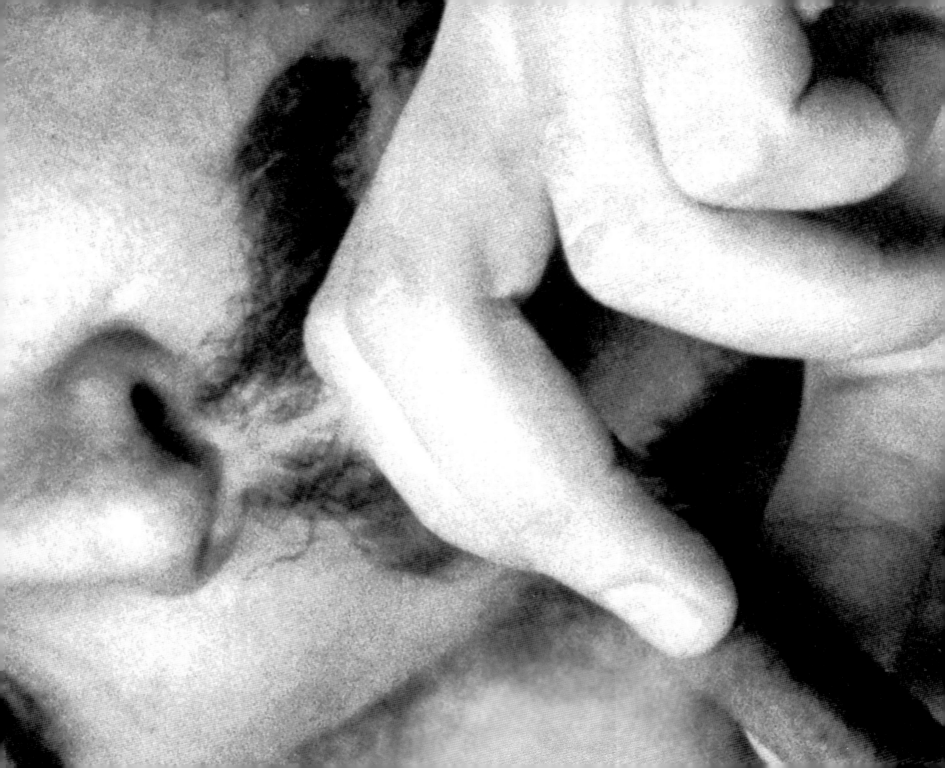

May 23, 1959

Dr. Miguel Ángel Quevedo,
Editor of *Bohemia*
Havana

Dear Sir,

Expecting from your traditional democratic spirit the respect for norms of freedom of the press, I am sending these lines in response to the miserable international crook who bears the splendid title of editor of the Latin American page of *Bohemia* magazine.

It is not my intention to defend myself against the fallacious imputations and the insidious reference to my Argentine citizenship. I am Argentine and I shall never renounce my country of origin (if you will excuse my historical boldness in the comparison, neither did Máximo Gómez renounce his Dominican homeland), but I feel Cuban, independently of whether the laws certify it or not: as a Cuban, I shared the sacrifices of the people throughout the armed struggle and today I share their hopes of bringing them to fruition. I am not a communist either (if I was, I would proclaim it to the four winds, just as I assert my demand as fighter for the causes of the people and reaffirm my hopes that the arms of the people of each oppressed country will clean the Latin American scene of all its trumped-up dictators). The fact is that the owners of Jules Dubois — United Fruit and other fruit, mining, livestock, telephone and electric companies, exploiters of the people — have given again the order to roll out the classic cover of their hirelings' lies.

Let neither slaves nor owners be deceived. Fidel Castro's words were irrevocable: "If they attack us, we shall arm even the cats." It is obvious, Mr. Dubois, that if the cats are to be armed, they have to be taught to use those arms, and don't think that you or the other lackeys who might come to this country will find a flock of frightened sheep. You will find a vibrant and united people that is disposed to fight an armed struggle right down to the last cartridge, as our prime minister stated in his last appearance before the press.

The soldiers of the revolution, beyond the different tactics that might exist at different times, are firmly united and no threat, no maliciousness, will be able to divide them in their struggle to achieve together the great goals of the people of Cuba: Agrarian Reform, Tariff Reform, Fiscal Reform, the translation of which means industrializing the country and bringing about the resulting improvements in the standard of living of the people, national liberation and international dignity.

Please receive my respects, Mr. Quevedo, although I cannot commend you on the jackal disguised as a sheep, whom you have permitted to appear in the pages of your magazine.

Ernesto Che Guevara
Commander-in-Chief R.M.A

to armando
hart

My dear secretary,

My congratulations for the opportunity they have given you to be God: you have six days for it. Before you finish and sit down to rest (unless you choose the wise road of the God before you, who rested earlier), I want to propose to you a few small ideas about the culture of our vanguard and of our people in general.

In this long vacation period I have had my nose buried in philosophy, something I've wanted to do for some time. I came across the first problem: nothing is published in Cuba, if we exclude the Soviet bricks which have the drawback of not letting you think, because the party has already done it for you and you just have to digest it. In terms of methodology, it is as anti-Marxist as can be and, moreover, the books tend to be very bad. Second, and no less important, was my ignorance of philosophical language (I fought hard with master Hegel and in the first round twice bit the dust). So I made a study plan for myself, which I think could be looked at and improved a lot, but it might constitute the basis for a real school of thought. We've achieved a lot but some day we'll have to think. My idea is a reading plan, naturally, but it could be expanded to bringing out serious works in the party publishing house.

If you take a look at your publications, you'll see the profusion of Soviet and French writers. This is because of the ease of obtaining translations and also ideological parrotry. This is not how to offer a Marxist culture to the people — at best it is Marxist teaching, which is necessary if the presentation is good (not the case), but insufficient.

My plan is this:

I. Philosophical classics

II. Great dialecticians and materialists

III. Modern philosophers

IV. Classics in economics and their precursors

V. Marx and Marxist thought

VI. Socialist construction

VII. Unorthodox thinkers and capitalists

VIII. Polemics

Left: Armando Hart (second from left).

Each series would be independent of the others and the program could be as follows:

I. Take the well-known classics that are already translated into Spanish, adding a serious preliminary study of a philosopher, Marxist if possible, and an ample explanatory vocabulary. A dictionary of philosophical terms would be published simultaneously, along with some history of philosophy. This could be Dennyk's and also Hegel's. Publication could be in a certain selective chronological order; in other words, start with one or two books of the greatest thinkers and continue the series through to the modern period, then go back to the past with other less important philosophers, and build on this with the tomes of the more representative ones, etc.

II. The same general model could be followed here, with compilations of some of the ancients (some time ago I read a study published in Argentina which included Democritus, Heraclitus and Leucippus).

III. The most representative modern philosophers could be published here, accompanied by serious and detailed studies by the experts (not necessarily Cuban) with the corresponding criticism of idealist points of view.

IV. This is being done now, but without any order and lacking the basic works of Marx. Here it would be necessary to publish the complete works of Marx and Engels, Lenin, Stalin and other great Marxists. For example, nobody has read anything of Rosa Luxemburg, who may have some errors in her criticism of Marx (Volume III) but they did kill her, and her instincts regarding imperialism are better than ours in some respects. There is also an absence of Marxist thinkers who later went off the rails, like Kautsky and Hilfering* (not spelt like that) who made some contributions, and many contemporary Marxists, who are not totally of the school.

V. Socialist construction. Books that deal with specific problems, not just of present leaders, but also of the past, with a serious scrutiny of the contributions of philosophers, and especially of economists and statisticians.

VI. Here would come the great revisionists (you can have Khrushchev here if you want), properly analyzed, and you should also have, in more depth than any other, your friend Trotsky, who, it seems, existed and wrote. Also the great theorists of capitalism, like Marshal, Keynes, Schumpeter, etc. These should also be carefully analyzed with explanations of the whys.

VII. As the heading suggests, this is the most polemical part, but that's how Marxist thought advanced. Proudhon wrote *The Philosophy of Poverty* and we know it exists because of [Marx's] *Poverty of Philosophy*. A critical edition might shed some light on the period and Marx's own development, which was still not complete. Robertus and Dühring belong to this period, and then came the revisionists and the big controversies of 1920 in the Soviet Union, which are perhaps the most important for us.

Now I can see that I skipped one section so the order's changed (my pen is flying here).

It would be Series IV, classics on economics and their precursors, which would include Adam Smith, the physiocrats, etc.

It's a gigantic job but Cuba deserves it and I think it can be attempted. I won't bother you anymore with this chatter. I've written to you because I don't know much about the people who are presently responsible for ideological orientation and it may not be prudent to write to them for other reasons (not just ideological parrotry, which also counts).

Okay, illustrious colleague (in the philosophical sense), I wish you success. I hope we can meet on the seventh day. A hug to the huggables, including one from me to your dear and feisty better half [Haydée Santamaría].

R.**

* Hilferding.

** Ramón was the pseudonym used by Che Guevara in the Congo in 1965. This letter was written from Africa.

toUNEAC

June 23, 1963
"Year of Organization"

UNEAC
Havana

Compañero,

No one can know to what point praise of himself is merited. Whatever the case, I don't like it and think it unnecessary.

I shall refer to some errors of content and form:

Content: My forbears who "showed signs of hatred for the oppressors of the people" were in fact members of the great Argentine cattle monopoly, and the struggle against Rosas was never mass-based.

Those who opposed Juan Manuel Rosas cannot be described as progressive from the Marxist point of view.

Incidentally, I was not socially engaged as an adolescent and nor did I participate in any political or student struggles in Argentina.

Form: This is not a book but a collection of notes.

Revolutionary greetings,
"Patria o Muerte. Venceremos."

Comandante Ernesto Che Guevara

to haydée

santamaría

Dear Yeyé,

Armando and Guillermo have told me about your tribulations. I respect and understand your decision but I would have liked to have hugged you personally instead of writing this letter. The security precautions here have been very strict and this has made it impossible for me to see many people I love (I am not as cold as I sometimes seem). I'm now seeing Cuba almost as if I'm a foreigner coming to visit: everything from a different angle. And this impression, despite my isolation, makes me understand the impression that visitors take away with them.

Thank you for the medical-literary parcels. I see you've become a woman of letters with the power of creation, but I confess that the way I like you best is on that day early in the new year, with all your fuses blown and firing volleys for miles around. This image and that of the Sierra (even our fights of those days are dear to my memory) are the ones of you I shall carry around with me for my own use. The affection and determination of all of you will help us in the difficult times that are approaching.

Your colleague

Who loves you

Left: Haydée Santamaría with
Fidel Castro in the Sierra Maestra, Cuba.

from raúl roa

December 19, 1963
Havana

Che,

Though it's very tardy I'm sending you a copy of the English version of your book *Guerrilla Warfare*.

If you want, I can use my good standing with Mao so that 600 million copies can be published in the language of Lao-Tse.

Best regards,
Raúl Roa

January 30
Cuban Embassy

My Viejito,

I'm writing you these lines to give you an idea of the trip and some feedback on your people as seen through the critical eye of this, your traveling ambassador.

Here you have your most solid team. It has personality and is organized but France is very neglected. Prensa Latina doesn't even have a Teletype and isn't receiving news in a place where it's happening every day and where it's increasingly important.

Papito's getting on with his creative syphilis, as some left-wing intellectual correctly described it. It might occur to him to flood the Sahara with water from Almendares but then he'd later need a team to do the engineering. In view of the political importance and the support Cuba has here among the people and in the government, we need more people here. We need to look for people in the party for the Cuba-Algeria committee, which is deserted, plus a few more for the embassy, as well as people for Foreign Trade, who could make a start and learn to work with pesetas until the time to deal in pounds sterling,

Left: Raúl Roa (left) with
Che Guevara and Aleida March.

His Excellency Carrillo has things under control. He's competing with the official poet publishing verses in French (Parnassian... and bad). It all comes out in *L'Essor*, the Bamaco paper [in Mali], which makes the *Gaceta de Mayajigua* (Mayajigua Gazette) look like the *New York Times*. He knows a great deal about the leaders and is well-liked, independently of some character defects. He's prepared to put himself on the line so they can use his experience in the most important places, but I think he's fine where he is, and he might well become the poet of the Sahara.

The underlings are two perfect corn-fed types but they function at the level required of them.

The analysis of Guinea was perfect. I read his reports and they exactly reflect the situation. He's very intelligent and I think he works better at his specific tasks, but he's totally lacking in any initiative in overcoming the coldness there is (better said, was) and in making contact with the masses of Guinean people. I have a temporary proposal for him, before he's sent out again, and that is to finish his degree studies in Havana. I'll tell you about it later. Besides, we need to name an ambassador who's a politician and who makes more contact with the people (not a good idea to have him for the reasons outlined). I spoke at length and frankly with Sékou Touré. He seems to be the clearest and most accomplished of the heads of government I've met in this part of Africa.

The Congo is a Bayú* with a president but the people are well-intentioned and, if a political team were sent, it could help a lot in getting them on the right track and avoiding a political coup, which is looming.

Ghana is the most developed of these countries, but there is a high degree of imperialist penetration. The ambassador is a bit of a cretin and he likes criticism about as much as you like Olivares, but he's serious, hardworking and studious. He runs the embassy confidently but I think that he should come back to Cuba within the year and work at something productive, in contact with our own surroundings, to rid him of certain ambassadorial habits that soften up people's revolutionary possibilities. The team pulls together well, at least from the outside. There's a commercial attaché who does nothing in his own field but who's always willing to help and he shines in one sense: he speaks English quite fluently.

Dahomey is another dump. The president and his vice-president are at loggerheads. There are many reasons for this. The president is progressive, as far as it goes here, but the vice is reactionary; the president is from Porto Novo, one of the capitals, but the vice is from Cotonú; the president is from one tribe and the vice from another; and we must never forget about bloody ambition. The president, who isn't the head of the executive (the vice is), wants to go to Cuba, and I think he should be invited. If they gave the go-ahead to Entralgo and the money could be spent, I'd recommend that Gonzalo Sala come as head of business to represent us there directly, after sending a shrewd ambassador to Guinea.

These are my superficial impressions. I'm writing them personally and I hate this gadget so I'll tell you more within the month when I get back. The itinerary so far is the following: China, Cairo, Khartoum, Dar es Salaam, and Algeria to attend an Afro-Asian conference on economics (as observer, at the personal invitation of Ben Bella). We must keep an eye on Syria: they're stirring things up.

Greetings to the bureaucratic, shortsighted mob around you and a cosmic embrace.

Che

* Land of sorcerers.

T his is the brief and intense exchange of letters between the "failed poet" Che confessed to harboring within himself and the "great, desperate poet," as he lovingly and admiringly described León Felipe.

Words are unnecessary. This is the domain of observation, but also of poetry, which moves here through the verses, letters and fragments of discourse. There is little to say about this dialogue which after three decades still preserves its original freshness and wisdom.

Let us only say, then, that this form of debate, based on poetry, bringing together respect, admiration and differing opinions into a single discussion, is yet another teaching from Che the witness.

—VC

thisismytributeand
ibegyoutointerpret
itassuch....

August 21, 1964
"Year of the Economy"

Sr. León Felipe,
Editorial Grijalbo S.A.
Avenida Granjas 82
México 16, D.F.

Maestro,

Some years ago, after the revolution came to power, I received your most recent book with a dedication written by yourself.

I never thanked you for it, but it has always been with me. It may interest you to know that one of the two or three books I have at my bedside is *El Ciervo* (The Deer), even though I have had little occasion to read it because, in Cuba, sleeping, having free time on one's hands, or resting, are simply sins of lese-leadership.

The other day I attended an event of great significance for me. The hall was packed with enthusiastic workers and there was a feeling present of the new man. A drop of the failed poet that I carry within me came to the surface and I had recourse to you, to engage with you at a distance. This is my tribute and I beg you to interpret it as such.

If the challenge tempts you, this invitation is sufficient.

With sincere admiration and esteem.

Comandante Ernesto Che Guevara

to turn everyday life into fire

...If you will permit me, I shall "thrust" a bit of poetry at you all. Don't worry, it is not of my own inspiration, as they say! It's a poem, just a few verses of a poem, by a desperate man. It is written by an old poet who is approaching the end of his life. He is more than 80 years old and saw many years ago the fall of the Spanish Republic, the political cause he fought for, and since then he's been in exile. Today he lives in Mexico. In his latest book, published some years ago, there are some interesting verses. He says:

...But man is a toiling and stupid child
who has made of work a long and sweaty day,
has made of the drumstick a hoe,
and has not played on the earth a song of joy
but instead began to dig...

Then he says, more or less, for my memory isn't very good:

I mean to say that no one has yet been able to dig
to the rhythm of the sun,
no one has cut an ear of corn
with love and grace.

This is precisely the attitude of the defeated from another world, a world we have already left behind through our attitude to work, through our desire to return to nature, to turn everyday life into fire.

I'm writing to you as a very slow old man

Mexico, March 27, 1965

My dear friend, Che Guevara,

I am writing to you as a very slow, old man but I owe you an embrace and I do not want to take my leave without giving it to you. So a friend of mine, Bertha, wife of an old friend, who holds you in the highest esteem, is bringing it for you.

I am sending you as a memento the autographed copy of the last poem I wrote a few days ago.

I wish you health and happiness.

With the esteem of your old friend,

Léon Felipe

The letter is written in the nimble handwriting which we later recognize in the *Bolivian Diary*. Even from the days of his restless, itinerant youth, his handwriting had accompanied Ernesto Guevara with an impressive loyalty. A reciprocal loyalty, let me be clear...

This man trusted words with the secrets of his battles; he asked them for nuances and advice to help him analyze his enemies and his friends, he demanded their presence at the moment of victory or in the times of discouragement he hardly ever confessed.

In this, he writes a letter of love for his children, from a great distance and in great haste. In it he offers affection and advice to all his children, asking for the girls' cooperation and inviting the boys, in the future, to fight or take a vacation to the moon, depending on the fate of the enemy. It is both a letter and a farewell, accompanied by an unpublished photograph of Che the witness, who appears here clean-shaven, carrying his daughter Celita, just before his next battle.

—VC

I to children

my

Above: With Celita, Pinar del Río, Cuba, 1966.

write to you from far away and in great haste

My dearest Aliusha, Camilo, Celita and Tatico,

I write to you from far away and in great haste, which means I can't tell you about my latest adventures. It's a pity, because I've met some very interesting friends through Pepe Caimán. * Another time...

Right now I want to tell you that I love you all very much and I remember you always, along with mamá, although the younger ones I almost only know through photos, as they were very tiny when I left. In a minute I'm going to get a photo taken so that you know how I look these days — a little bit older and uglier.

This letter should arrive about the time Aliusha has her sixth birthday, so may it serve to congratulate her and hope that she has a very happy birthday.

Aliusha, you should study hard and help your mother in everything you can. Remember, you are the oldest.

Camilo, you should swear less as in school you shouldn't speak like that and you have to learn what is appropriate. Celita, help your grandmother around the house as much as you can and continue being as sweet as when we said goodbye — do you remember? How could you not. Tatico, you should grow and become a man so that later we'll see what you make of yourself. If imperialism still exists, we'll set out to fight it. If it is finished, you, Camilo and I will take a vacation on the moon.

Give a kiss from me to your grandparents, to Miriam and her baby, to Estela and Carmita, and here's an elephant-sized kiss from...

Papá

*Pepe the Crocodile, a Cuban saying for Uncle Sam.

Note in the margin:

To Hildita [Che's oldest daughter], another elephant-sized kiss and tell her I'll write soon, but now I don't have time.

he *Stone* is an impressive story written by Che in the Congo.

In its original unpublished version, from which this is excerpted, it occupies 10 pages of his notebook, written with few corrections.

The theme of the story — contemplating the possible death of Celia, his mother — situates the writing at some point after May 22, 1965. On that day, Osmany Cienfuegos gave Che "the saddest news of the war, that in a telephone conversation from Buenos Aires they said my mother is very ill, in a tone suggesting that this was simply a preparatory announcement... I had to spend a month in this unhappy uncertainty, waiting to hear something I guessed was happening, but still hoping that there was some mistake in the news, until confirmation came of my mother's death."

In the midst of "this unhappy uncertainty," Che constructed a story highly introspective in tone, bringing together philosophical reflection, irony, pain and tenderness. It is likely the most raw, intense and moving story that he wrote.

Beyond attempting here, in a few words, an analysis of the text from any of the possible angles, we feel satisfied and honored that this book includes this essential document of Che the witness. It outlines, in particularly dramatic circumstances, features of his personality and writing that bring us, readers at a distance, closer to the kind of solitude so deeply felt at the time by the author, for all his impressive human stature.

The scope of a personality, its capacity for communication, is also measured in the territories of thought and daily matters it can simultaneously encompass.

It is also possible to appreciate here the philosophical density of the story *Doubt*, and the tenderness of the postcards sent to his children from Africa. This same voice, in the formidable and terrible circumstances of action, is capable of modulation through word, tone and image.

Other words to other people, dedications Che wrote in books he was giving away, do justice to friendship, admiration and solidarity.

The man who wrote them also left evidence of the importance of the matter to hand and its transcendence, in these words taken from an impressive story: "One survives in the species, in history, in that mystified form of life, in acts, in memories."

—VC

AFRICA: winds from the west and breezes from the east

mydreamsare
withoutlimits...
(bookdedications)

On the road from Dar-Es-Salaam to Kigoma, Tanzania, 1965.

To Cesáreo Rivero

For Cesáreo Rivero, wishing him a happy Capablanca.*

Che

To Don Tomás Roig

Don Tomás, I heard about your interest in this book of *Plantas Medicinales* (Medicinal Plants) from *compañero* Cid, and I am pleased to deliver it to you now.

I beg you to consider it a small tribute from this ministry to a scientist who raised the profile of Cuba before the revolution made it universally known.

In addition, please accept my personal homage, as a man who has experienced the tense peace of the retort stand and who sometimes yearns for that former individual trade, although he gave nothing to humanity from that trench.

Respectfully,

Che

To José Manuel Manresa

For Manresa, here where the paths bifurcate (temporarily?). With one last handshake.

To Alberto Granado**

My mobile home will continue to have two legs and my dreams will be without limits... at least until the bullets have the last word.

Sedentary gipsy, I expect to see you when the smell of gunfire has died away. A hug for all of you.

Che

* A famous Cuban chess championship.

** Granado was Che's companion on his early travels through Latin America.

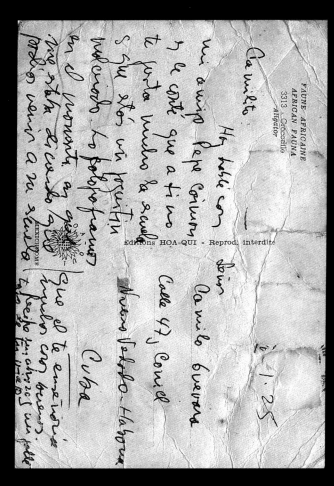

Camilito:

Today I spoke with my friend Pepe Caimán and I told him that you didn't like school very much and that you're just a teeny bit spoiled. We took a photo of him at the exact moment when he was telling me he could come to your school, and that he'd teach you lots of good things.

Receive a hug and a big slap from your old man.

Dear little one:

I was watching the little gazelles run across the savannah and I remembered you. Nothing more, except here there are lions and in our country the little gazelles will be able to run without anyone chasing them.

Don't forget to go to school and give a kiss to your new brother in my name.

A kiss from papá

Señorita
Alicia Baeora
Calle 47 y Coral
Nuevo Vedado – Habana
CUBA

Gravilita:

Con perdito eros por la zabra y me acorde de ti. Nada mas que aqui hay leones en …

AFRICAN WILD LIFE · THOMSONS GAZELLA

Copyright by Sapra Studio P.O. Box 5882, Nairobi

He gave me the news as such things must be said to a strong person, one in charge, and for that I was grateful. He did not lie about his concern or his pain, while I tried not to show either. It was that simple!

Besides, I had to wait for confirmation before I could officially be in mourning. I wondered if one could cry a little. No, no, it was not possible, the boss is impersonal — not that he's denied the right to feel but simply that he must not show what he feels about his own affairs; those of his soldiers, maybe.

"It was a friend of the family, calling to say she was seriously ill, but I wasn't there that day."

"Seriously — you mean dying?"

"Yes."

"Be sure to tell me if there's anything else."

"As soon as I hear, but there's no hope. I don't think so."

Death's messenger had gone but I had no confirmation. To wait was all I could do. I'd decide when the news became official whether or not I had the right to express my grief. I was inclined to think not.

The morning sun struck hard after the rain. There was nothing strange in it — every day it rained and then the sun came out to impose itself and drive away the damp. In the afternoon, the stream would be crystalline once again, although not much water had fallen in the mountains this day; this was almost usual.

They said that on May 20 it stopped raining and wouldn't rain again until October.

They said... but they say so many things that aren't true.

Will nature be guided by the calendar? I didn't care whether or not this was the case. In general, I didn't care about anything at all, about this forced inactivity, about this idiot war without aims. Well, maybe it had aims. But they were so vague, so diluted, that they seemed unattainable, like some surrealist inferno where tedium is the eternal punishment. And, besides, I did care. Of course I cared.

I have to find some way of breaking out of this, I thought. Easy to think. One could make a thousand plans, each as tempting as the next, then choose the best, fuse two or three together to make one, simplify it, put it on paper and hand it in. That was the end of it and then one started anew. An unusually intelligent form of bureaucracy: instead of filing anything, make it disappear. My men said they smoked it. Any bit of paper can be smoked if there's something inside it.

It was an advantage, in that what I didn't like could be changed in the next plan. Nobody would notice. It seemed like this could go on for eternity.

I felt like smoking and took out my pipe. It was, as always, in my pocket. Unlike my soldiers, I never lost my pipes. It was very important for me to have it. One can travel any distance along paths of smoke; I would say that plans can be created and victory dreamed without it seeming like a dream, but more like reality made vaporous with the distance and the mist that is always there in smoke trails. It's a very good companion, a pipe. How could they lose something so necessary? What brutes!

They were not brutes. They had their activity and were exhausted from that activity. So they didn't have to think, and what use is a pipe unless for thinking? One can dream. Yes, one can dream, but the pipe is important when one dreams from afar, dreaming toward a future whose only path is smoke, or dreaming back to a past that is so distant it is necessary to retrace one's steps. Immediate yearnings are felt elsewhere in the body. They have vigorous feet and keen eyes and they do not need help from smoke. My soldiers lost their pipes because they were not essential to them: things that are essential are not lost.

Do I have anything else like that? The gauze scarf. That was different: she gave it to me in case I injured my arm, in which case it would make a loving sling. The problem would be if I cracked open my skull. But there would be a simple solution: I could wind it around my head to tie up my jaw and then I'd take it to the tomb with me. Loyal even in death. But if I was left lying on the mountain or if somebody else picked me up, there'd be no gauze scarf. I'd decompose on the grass or they might exhibit me; maybe I'd even appear in *Life* magazine, my desperate death gaze fixed at a moment of extreme fear. Because one is afraid. Why deny it?

Above: Reading, Congo, 1965.

238 239

Through the smoke, I followed old trails and reached the intimate corners of my fears, always linked to death, this disturbing and inexplicable nothingness, however much we Marxist-Leninists describe death with such conviction as just nothingness. And what is this nothingness? Nothing. The simplest and most convincing explanation possible. Nothing is nothing, shut down your brain, dress it in black robes if you like, with a sky of distant stars. That is what nothingness is: nothing. Equivalent to infinity.

One survives in the species, in history, that mystified form of life, in acts, in memories. Have you never felt shivers run down your spine reading of Maceo's machete charges? That is life after nothingness. And our children. I wouldn't want to live on in my children: they don't even know me. I am just a foreign body occasionally disturbing their peaceful existence, getting between them and their mother.

I imagined my oldest child, and she, with gray in her hair, saying reproachfully, "Your father would not have done this. Or that." Inside myself, son of my father, I felt a tremendous sense of rebellion. As a son, I would not know whether it was true that, as a father, I would have done such-and-such a thing, or done it badly. But as my son, I would feel vexed and betrayed that this memory of I, a father, had been thrown in my face all the time. My son had to become a man, nothing more, not better or worse, just a man. I was grateful to my father for his sweet and unselfrighteous displays of affection. And my mother? Poor old woman. Officially, I did not yet have the right to mourn her and had to await the confirmation.

I wandered like this along these trails of smoke when a soldier interrupted me, pleased to be useful.

"You haven't lost anything?"

"Nothing," I said, associating this particular nothing with the other of my reverie.

"Check."

I felt my pockets. Everything in order.

"Nothing."

"And this little stone? I saw it on your key ring."

"I'll be damned!"

I was hit savagely by self-reproach. One loses nothing that is necessary, nothing vital. Is one alive if things are no longer necessary? As a vegetable yes, but as a moral being, no, at least I don't believe so.

I felt the chill of memory and found myself, rigorous, meticulous, feeling my pockets while the water flowed past, brown with the mountain soil and keeping its secret from me. The pipe, first of all the pipe: it was there. The papers or the scarf would have floated. The vaporizer present; pens here; notebooks in their nylon covers, yes; the matchbox, also present. All in order. The chill dissolved.

I had brought only two small keepsakes into battle, the gauze scarf from my wife and the key ring with the stone in it from my mother, a cheap and ordinary thing. The stone had come loose and I kept it in my pocket.

Did that stream flow with mercy or vengeance, or was it simply impersonal, like a boss? Does one not cry because one must not or because one cannot? Is there no right to forget, even in war? Is it necessary to conceal ice beneath macho clothing?

I don't know. I really don't know. I know only that I have a physical need for my mother to appear, to rest my head in her bony lap and for her to say "my darling," with such tenderness, to feel her clumsy hand in my hair, caressing me like a wind-up doll, as if the tenderness was streaming only from her eyes and her voice, the broken channels no longer bearing it to the extremities. The hands tremble and touch rather than caress, but the tenderness still slips out to surround them, and one feels so good, so small, so strong. There is no need to ask her for forgiveness. This is evident in her words "my darling"...

"Do you find it strong? It affects me too. Yesterday I nearly fell over when I tried to stand up. Looks like they didn't dry it properly."

"It's shit. I'm waiting on the order to see if they bring some cut tobacco that's halfway decent. One has a right to smoke, even just a quiet and pleasant-tasting pipe, don't you think...?"

doubt

"No. The bull, no way…"

With barely a trace of the vague uneasiness hidden deep within, and permitting his confident smile to appear unhindered, he observed the scene.

He was watching the fierce bull with its threatening horns; it knew no limits to its freedom other than the frail stick of the cowherd, and now pawed the bare ground in surprise and pain. One could see it was overwhelmed by rage, and that it was ready to attack.

He had to acknowledge to himself that he wanted to see the soldier rolling on the ground, his body just slightly bloodied. Not that he wished for something terrible to happen to him, not completely terrible, but that the situation should have already been resolved by now.

The soldier was smiling, confidence emanating from every pore. He was looking at the bull with such a mocking air that it stabbed through the heart.

He was within range. Just one shot would do the job.

These men were black, but they were different. One sensed that they felt superior. As if their ancestors' journey across the ocean had given them a new strength, a greater knowledge of worldly things. That was all very well (the commissar was forever repeating that attention to progress and science was vital for the construction of a new world), but why should the ancient wisdom of the mountains be ignored that way? How could they now laugh disdainfully at these forces that made them invulnerable to enemy bullets?

He felt a slight itching in the scar and scratched it lightly as if wanting to cast off that inappropriate memory. The keloid maintained a stubborn presence and he scratched harder, carefully skirting the still painful scar.

He was ashamed to confess it at first, but he had felt it was nobler to speak. They were all blaming the Muganga,* threatening him, but he confessed, and asked that the others confess as well.

In fact, the fear had come upon him even before they reached the position. The jungle has many strange and sinister noises. One never knows if it is some wild beast that will suddenly leap out, or a snake, or some forest spirit. And, furthermore, there was the enemy waiting at the end of the track.

He remembered the anguish rising in waves in his throat as the clarity of the sky announced the dawn… and the trembling all over his body, which he had attributed to the cold while knowing that it was not the cold, as the waiting crushed them, and he no longer knew which was greater: the fear of fighting, or the fear of waiting.

The red flash exploded over the trenches where the enemy should have been, even before the rattling could be heard. Then all hell broke loose, bringing with it the curious sensation of being unafraid. Without even realizing it, the trembling had left him and he proudly noted how the short flashes traveled straight from his gun, not tracing those grotesque arches — like a ceiling over the enemy's head — that he could see all around him.

"They're shooting with their eyes closed. They haven't learned anything," he thought.

Then he heard a slight whistling sound and a great din, as if the earth were breaking open; then came a cloud of smoke and dust, and another, and another. He looked to his left after the last explosion, closer than the earlier ones, and saw his comrade lying in a strange position: one hand trapped by his body, moving as if trying to break free, beating a strange rhythm identical to that of the head doubled over the chest.

In the dawn light he glimpsed a pair of clouded eyes, like those of a goat with its throat cut. He observed that with each movement a small spurt of blood flowed from under the chin and that the blood was staining the earth, sticking to the beard as sparse as a goat's…

It was then that the trembling returned, but different from before. Previously, it had been a contest with his willpower, but now it seemed to compel him to take flight… And then he remembered he'd left his gun behind; he was trying to flee, to escape that hell and save himself, and it seemed as though the trees were pushing him back or holding him there with their clinging branches, trying to wrench him away from life, from the horrific symphony of bullets and the strange cracking noise… At first, there was only the cracking, like something coming from his body. He didn't even relate it to his fall, which he attributed to the branches of the enemy trees.

He only realized he was wounded when he tried to run again. That was the darkest part of his memories. Until then, he had been running at the same speed as his fear, which had melted into him, become one with him, so that he no longer felt it so strongly. Now his fear had overtaken him, and was itself running through the tangled vegetation, but it didn't want to go on alone, so it turned back and pulled at him. At that moment he felt all the anguish of the dissociation and tried to keep walking, only to fall with a groan. His fear tired of waiting for him and fled alone, leaving him stretched out on the barely visible path, only groaning now, with a tortured, withering calm because his fear had now gone.

Yes, it was true that Dawa** protected. While he had been in control of his fear, nothing had happened to him; he was only wounded when he fled, prey to panic.

He was indignant that his comrades were so false as to deny this, holding the inefficiency of the Muganga responsible for everything.

There had certainly been no opportunity to even touch a woman and the honor of the dead could be affirmed, but did not fear perhaps exist? They all knew it very well: if they touched a woman, or took an object that was not theirs, or if they were afraid, Dawa was no longer effective.

He had been the only one brave enough to admit it to the angry mob: he had been afraid. They had also felt fear, and they should recognize the fact.

It irritated him to remember the gesture of contained rage made by that little man who had been wounded in the neck. He had denied his fear with such hypocritical vehemence! With such great irreverence, eyes blazing, he had accused the Muganga of being a puppet, although he never moved his head, which seemed to be held in the grip of two powerful hands.

He felt satisfied for having imposed some discipline with nothing more than his confession and his stance. The foreigners, who did not boast so much, also had their dead and wounded from other fighting, though their Dawa must have been more powerful since they didn't need to go through all the motions before each battle. But they were selfish people and smilingly denied that they had it, even denied it to the commander. He had heard how the latter humbly asked the leader of the foreigners for their Dawa, and how the leader had laughed as if he'd heard some funny story and jabbered something in his semi-language about consciousness, and internationalism, and how all of us brothers... Yes, close brothers, but they weren't going to let their Dawa go.

The chicken episode had confused him a little. The Muganga (yet another new one, because the commander had been weak enough to give in and replace the previous one) had prepared everything with great care, assuring them that it was invulnerable. But with the first shot the chicken had been killed good and dead, and the foreigners had eaten it right before the scandalized gaze of the fighters.

But now — this bull: if only it would trap that arrogant man between its horns and show him the power of Dawa! Or, at least, if it would get away unharmed, for it was too miserable to wish harm upon a brother who had got him out of the combat zone when everyone else was running away, and who had organized his transfer to the hospital.

He had bad memories of the hospital. First, the white doctors who laughed because the bullet had gone through his buttocks, as if he could choose where they were going to wound him. And when he'd told them he'd been wounded because he was afraid, they laughed even more. These whites were nasty; with their color and their science they felt they could laugh at everything — superior to everything around them. For a moment he had wished he'd been left, dead, there where the bullet had found him. Then he wouldn't have had to suffer such humiliation. But what would have become of the Muganga then?

In the soldier, who was aiming at the fierce bull with all the insolence of a conquistador, he could not recognize the human being, the friend, the brother who had helped him escape that hell. How that noble face had contracted when a shadow of his own tribe had passed by his side without turning its head, without helping him. How one could divine in him the crude words, daughters of a beautiful sun. The brother had turned conquistador, looking on them from the heights of a distant mountain like some god or demon.

But that contraction was so different from the one on the soldier's face now, beneath the powerful sun. The

The little man with the bullet wound in the neck had wanted them to kill the Muganga and they would have been capable of doing so had he not intervened. Good thing he had lived. In short, one had to be honest, one had to recognize that to have fear is bad.

But the little man with the bullet wound in the neck said he had seen many people fleeing in terror and that nothing had happened to them. That was the most cowardly among them, those who had stayed behind without participating, were also safe and sound. He said that he himself had not been afraid and that his wound was a mortar wound (because it was at the back of the neck, in the nape). The whites said it didn't look like a mortar wound, but the little man argued that the bullet had gone through him. Yet his wound was in the nape of his neck and if it had really been a bullet it would have blown his head off.

The little man with the bullet wound in the neck argued a lot. It seemed that he'd learned this from the whites. One felt uncomfortable when he was speaking. He'd say, for example, "If Dawa doesn't protect those who are afraid, and all of us are afraid, then what use is Dawa?"

He replied that you have to believe in Dawa, but the little man said no, Dawa had to give you that faith, otherwise it was of no use.

This little man with the bullet wound in the neck talked a lot, but he stayed behind in hospital and didn't want to return to the front. When he said goodbye, he made the little man feel his cowardice in staying; it was a kind of revenge…

The bang pulled him out of his mists and everything shook because he wasn't expecting it. The bull looked around stupidly, sank to its knees on the ground and began to tremble with its dull eyes staring directly at him.

"Just like the goat… and that man," he thought.

He hardly felt the foreigner's approving pat on the back, but the strident laugh wounded him like a knife. A great somnolence overcame him; he didn't want to think about anything.

As they walked together, the Muganga told him that the foreigners were good friends and had proved as much. He looked at him in surprise. The Muganga explained in a paternal tone that Dawa saved them from their enemies, but never from the weapon of a friend. That was why the bull had died, and the friendship of the foreigners had therefore been demonstrated.

With these explanations, the boy felt as if something was lifted from him, that a great burden he had been carrying had been removed. But somehow it also ensured he would never be totally free of the burden and, in a still undefined way, something sharper, a new and insatiable monster began to stir in his depths: doubt.

* Muganga: The man who administered the magic Dawa rites that protected the soldiers against bullets.

** Dawa: The magic forces of a ritual to make men invulnerable to bullets.

Above: At the main camp. Congo, 1965.

t is not too difficult to deal with this theme, because the man we are talking about left us words that would become a clear declaration of his principles.

In the second part of his *Episodes from the Revolutionary War: Congo*, taking stock of what he had got right and what he had got wrong in his involvement, Che confessed: "...my two basic weaknesses were satisfied in the Congo: tobacco, which I almost always had, and reading, which was always abundant."

It is true: reading accompanied this man throughout his life, as an essential source of knowledge and as a gift he enjoyed by slaking an intense intellectual and spiritual thirst.

It is also true that the persistence of his reading was matched by his capacity for memory and analysis. In his personal archive today are still preserved the first lists of the books he devoured in his youth. The record of titles and authors reveals the wide scope of the young reader's cultural interests.

Philosophy, history, literature, sports and the sciences appear among the favorite themes of the youthful Ernesto. Poetry moves through this enviable catalogue, with works from the extraordinary *La Divina Commedia* through to Milton's *Paradise Lost*, absorbed through the eyes of this avid reader, who then incorporated what he had read by systematically writing and keeping notes on his reading. These literary criticisms are a testimony to the effect his reading had on him from the beginning, and years later can be used to evaluate what he read (and perhaps the reader himself).

I believe that the underlying feature of Che's literary consumption and his reflections on what he read, is love. Though it is not always confessed (or even recognized), there is a loving, intimate, irreplaceable relationship between the reader who enjoys and needs such an emancipatory act, and the book that offers joy and sadness, questions, answers and more questions, anxieties and celebrations. There is also a visual testimony of Che's love of reading, in photographs: Che with a book in hand, in the African jungle, in his ministerial office or throughout the guerrilla war in Bolivia. If there are no photographs of this insatiable reader in the tranquility of his Havana home, it is surely because his time in Cuba was filled with multiple tasks and pressing demands. We know that he left a soundtrack of this love of words: Che made a tape recording of the poems of several authors he used to read to his wife Aleida, leaving it with her when he went off to fight in his final mission.

The names of his favorite writers can be extracted from these notes he happily wrote and kept, without knowing it, for us. If echoes of the powerful and communicative voice of Nicolás Guillén animated their family readings, Che's written notes proclaim his poetic tastes: the Peruvian César Vallejo and the Chilean Pablo Neruda, two greats of 20th century Latin American poetry, appear among other writers he comments on. Vallejo, in this case, after his work as a journalist and witness in his *Russia in 1931*, and Neruda, with more extensive comments on his exuberant *Canto General*, a book that accompanied the guerrilla fighter in his pack to the Bolivian jungle.

—VC

an insatiable

Reader:

an insatiable literary criticisms

vicentesáenz's martí:rootsand wingsofthecuban liberator

This is a small portrait of the liberator, with heavy quotations, giving an idea of the clear and elegant thought of the revolutionary poet.

One could not say it is a masterpiece, but that's not its function either. Simply, the author is overwhelmed by Martí's words, which are sufficient in themselves to clarify the concepts at hand. The author limits himself to ordering them more or less chronologically, until the time of Martí's death.

If the booklet has something, though, it is the final comparison with certain run-of-the-mill contemporary politicians.

To describe Rómulo Betancourt or Haya de la Torre as equals of Martí is an insult to the man who lived in the belly of the beast and knew its entrails, though they were not nearly as black and pestilent then as they are now. The book would be much better without this final invocation.

Above: In his Havana home, Cuba, 1964.

carlos fallas's
mamita yunai

This book was written by a worker as his entry in the competition for best Latin American novel of 1940. The Costa Rican jury, "considering that this account could not be taken as a novel, disqualified it." This appears in the note ending the book as a kind of colophon, and from a technical point of view maybe the jury was right, because this story is not a true novel. But it is a vital account written in the depths of the forest, and it basks in the warmth of "welcoming" Mamita Yunai, the United Fruit Company, whose tentacles drain the sap of the people of Central America and of still others in South America.

The story is clear, dry and simply written. The first part describes the narrator's vicissitudes overseeing some elections, with all the dirty tricks that were played, until he returns to Limón and meets with an old friend on the

way. This meeting leads into the flashback of the second part: his adventures on a banana plantation and the injustice and robbery of the company until one of his coworkers tries to kills a *tútile* [sic], an Italian in the pay of La Yunai, and who goes to prison.

The third part, a kind of epilogue in the form of a dialogue between the two, describes their lives in the intervening period, ending with the two men going their separate ways: the author, who narrates in first person the struggles for political demands, and his friend to the La Yunai banana plantations.

There is no doubt that the main character is the author, and he is right not to mix himself up with the people he's writing about. He sees them suffering, he understands and sympathizes, but he does not identify

with them. He is witness rather than actor. He knows the places he is writing about and it is clear he has considerable experience of them. The psychology of his coworkers and the anecdotes he includes fit well with the text, though there are times when the latter seem a little out of place in the story.

As always with this kind of novel, there is no psychological complexity in the characters, in particular in the "machos" (gringos), who are like "bad guy" cardboard cutouts.

When his recriminations become howls just for effect, he falls into the commonplace of Latin American novels, but the book is, above all, a notable and vivid document describing the outrages of the company and the "authorities," and the wretched lives of the railway workers (on the lines), to whom the book is dedicated.

*Guard.

Left: Congo, 1965.

césar vallejo's
russia in 1931

The great Peruvian poet takes a look here at Russia at the time of its construction, one of the most controversial times in its history, the year 1931 when the first Five Year Plan was underway.

Vallejo tackles the problem as a whole and does not flinch from describing the poverty, the flaws and the different kinds of opposition, but all this, along with the results of more recent years, makes it all the more necessary to tell the entire story.

He situates himself as a sympathizer without party affiliations, but his glossy Marxist analysis still gives him away as a bourgeois who came to communism. Leaving aside the pompous Latin American custom of practising poetry even in the bathroom, Vallejo is an accurate reporter whose vignettes of the Russian reality are written with the precision of a photographic lens.

There are moments when one suspects the impartiality of this reporter was drowned by the enthusiasm of the militant, for example when he lists chess among the parlor games banned by the Soviets, for today they are the indisputable champions. But one must also take into account the fact that the conditions of life have changed fundamentally in Soviet society and that it is most proud of this change. Precisely because of this, and with all the anxieties of the production fever of 1931, it is not surprising that chess was regarded as a pernicious luxury.

In short, this book consolidates the faith of those who have it, but I don't know what impression it would make on those who don't.

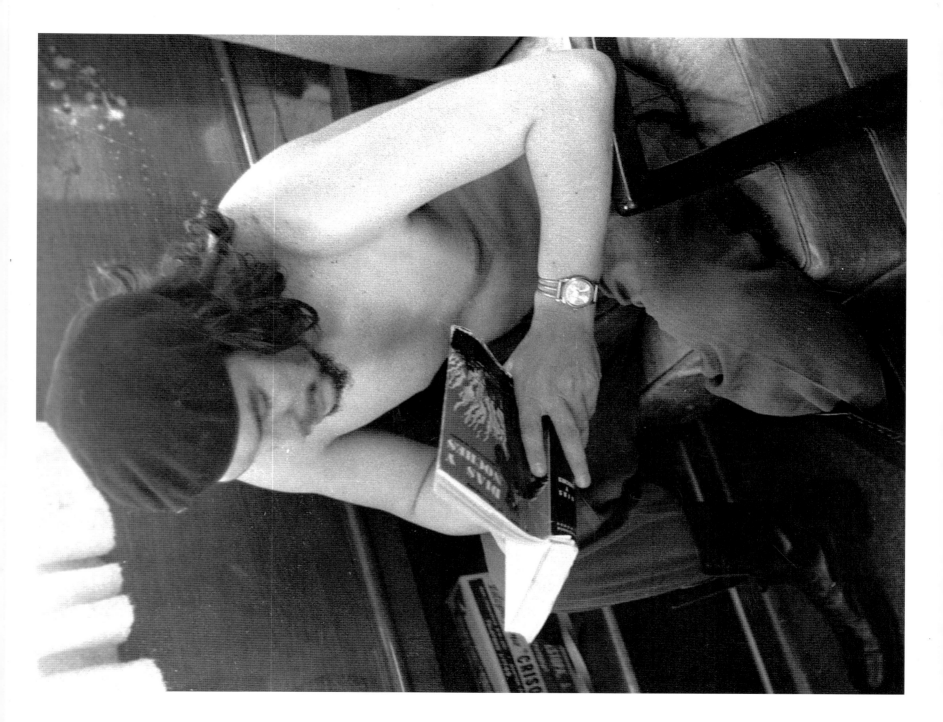

pabloneruda's cantogeneral

When time has smoothed over these political events a little and has equally, ineluctably, given the people their definitive victory, this book of Neruda's will appear as the greatest symphonic poem of the Americas.

It is poetry constituting a milestone and possibly a summit. Everything in it, even the few (inferior) verses at the end breathe its extraordinary significance. In it, the poet crystallizes the about-face he made when he stopped talking to himself and came down (or up) to speak with us, ordinary mortals, members of the mass of people.

It is the universal hymn of the Americas that retraces everything, from the geographic giants to the shameful little pets of Mr. Monopoly.

The first chapter is called "A Lamp on Earth" and one hears in it, among other things, his greeting to the immense Amazon.

Amazon
Capital of the water's syllables
patriarchal father...

A fitting metaphor joins the exact tones of Neruda's portrait, giving us the atmosphere, revealing to us its impact on him, so that he no longer sings as a subtle wanderer but as a man. It is precisely this first chapter of his description, which we could call pre-Columbian, that closes with "Men," our distant ancestors.

The mineral race was
like a cup of clay, man
made of stone and atmosphere,
clean as earthen jugs, sonorous.

The poet then finds the synthesis of what this Latin America of ours was, its greatest symbol, and he sings then to the "Heights of Macchu-Picchu." Macchu-Picchu is the work of indigenous engineering that speaks most to us, with its elegant simplicity, its graying sadness, the marvelous landscape that surrounds it and the River Urubamba howling below. His synthesis of Macchu-Picchu is achieved in three lines that are descriptions almost in the class of Goethe:

Mother of stone, seaspray of the condors.
Towering reef of the human dawn.
Spade lost in the primal sand.

He is not content merely with defining it and narrating its history so, in an episode of poetic madness, he pulls out of the hat all his dazzling and sometimes hermetic metaphors for the symbol-city, occasionally calling to it for help:

Give me silence, water, hope.
Give me struggle, iron, volcanoes.

What happened? We all know the sequence of the story. "The Conquistadors" appear on the horizon:

The butchers razed the islands.
Guanahaní was first
in this story of martyrdom.

Then come Cortés, Alvarado, Balboa, Ximénez de Queseda, Pizarro and Valdivia. All of them are pitilessly savaged by his song, which explodes like pistol fire. The only one for whom the poet has any kindly words is Ercilla, singer of the epic "Araucana":

Canto General

Pablo Neruda

Cuando el tiempo haya terminado en
los años poéticos) en
tiempo — inevitablemente l el mismo
pruebas su triunfo definitivo rigió
Este libro de Neruda como el más alto
poema sinfónico del América.

... Espero que nuestra un Hito s quizá
una cumbre Todo en ella, todo lo pro
(e inferior) cientos grandes del finer
re firma transcendental. se pese inteligir
se recobra vuelta Su Río. cuando a ...
transformar un diálogo en algo un uno
(y orquesta (o más una) a desde la con
nuestra, en mujeres en toda. En inte —
país del pueblo.
Es un esto personal de América
que de un novo a todo l nuestra
halla lo grande Pacífico toda es poder
todos pueblo del señor monopolio
El pu mar explica se llama de Europa
en la Tierra "... y esto estar ocurra un solo por
por el figueireco ameniza...
Pablo
Capital del b Bibar del gran,
Pedro Latinora

Marina Hemingway,
Cuba, 1960.

Worthy man, sonorous Ercilla, I hear the pulsing
water of your first dawn, a frenzy of birds
and a thunderclap in the foliage.
Leave, oh, leave your blond
eagle's imprint, crush
your cheek against the wild corn,
everything will be devoured in the dust.

Yet the conquest will continue and will mark its own stamp on the Americas, so that Neruda says, "Despite the Fury":

But through fire and horseshoe,
as from a fountain illuminated
by the somber blood,
with the metal engulfed by the tempest,
a light was cast over the earth:
number, name, line and structure.

...So with the cruel
titan of stone,
the death-dealing falcon,
not only blood but wheat arrived.

The light came despite the daggers.

But the long night of Spain comes to an end and the night of the monopolies looms. All the greats of the Americas have their place in this hymn, from the early liberators to the new; the priests who struggle side-by-side with the people. Now the sound of gunshot disappears and a great song immerses the reader in its joy and hope. In particular it dreams of the epic of the land, of Lautaro and his guerrilla fighters and Caupolicán, who was impaled. "Lautaro Against the Centaur (1554)" gives a clear idea:

Fatigue and death led
Valdivia's troops through the foliage.

Lautaro's spears drew near.

Amid corpses and leaves Pedro de Valdivia
advanced, as in a tunnel.

Lautaro came in the dark.

He thought about stony Extremadura,
about golden olive oil in the kitchen,
the jasmine left beyond the seas.

He recognized Lautaro's war cry.

...Valdivia saw the light coming, the dawn,
perhaps life, the sea.

        It was Lautaro.

The mysterious meeting of Guayaquil had to be included in the hymn, and in the lines of their political discussion, the spirits of the two great generals are palpitating. But it was not all the heroic and honorable struggle of these two generals. There were also betrayers, executioners, jailers and murderers. "The Sand Betrayed" opens with "The Hangmen."

Saurian, scaly America coiled
around vegetable growth, around the flagpole
erected in the swamp:
you nursed terrible children
with poisonous serpent's milk,
torrid cradles incubated
and covered a bloodthirsty
progeny with yellow clay.
The cat and the scorpion fornicated
in the savage land.

And the Rosas, the Francias, the García Morenos, appear and parade by, and not just names but institutions, castes and groups. Neruda asks his colleagues, "Celestial Poets":

What did you do, Gidists,
intellectualists, Rilkists,
mistificators, false existentialist
sorcerers, surrealist
butterflies burning
in a tomb, Europeanized
cadavers of fashion,
pale worms of capitalist
cheese…

And when he comes to the North American companies, his powerful voice exhales with sympathy for the victims and disgust and loathing for the octopuses and for all those who fragment and gobble up Our America.

When the trumpet sounded everything
on earth was prepared
and Jehovah distributed the world
to Coca-Cola Inc., Anaconda,
Ford Motors and other entities:
United Fruit Inc.
reserved for itself the juiciest,
the central seaboard of my land,
America's sweet waist.

To González Videla, the president who sent him into exile, Neruda shouts:

Wretched clown, miserable
mixture of monkey and rat, whose tail
is combed with gold pomade on Wall Street.

But neither has everything died, and his cry bursts forth from hope.

America, I do not invoke your name in vain.

He concentrates on his own country, with the "Canto General of Chile" in which, after describing it and singing to it, he offers his "Winter Ode to the Mapochu River."

O, yes, imprecise snow,
O, yes, trembling in full snowy blossom,
boreal eyelid, little frozen ray,
who, who called you to the ashen valley,
who, who dragged you from the eagle's beak
down to where your pure waters touch
my country's terrible tatters?

Then comes the land in "The Earth's Name is Juan" and, through the awkward singing of each worker, the song of Margarita Naranjo is heard, heartbreaking in its naked pathos.

I am dead. I am from María Elena.

The poet unleashes all his rage against the main guilty parties, against the monopolies, and he addresses his poem "Let the Woodcutter Awaken" to a Yankee soldier.

West of the Colorado River
there's a place that I love.

Right: Ñancahuasú, Bolivia, 1967.

He warns:

The world will be implacable for you.
Not only will the islands be deserted but the air
that now knows the words that it loves.

...And from the laboratory covered with vines
the unleashed atom will also set forth
toward your proud cities.

González Videla begins the persecution of Neruda, making of him "The Fugitive" and here his hymn loses
a little, for it is as if improvisation has found its pastures in his poetry so that the Canto's lofty metaphor loses height
and abandons its delicate rhythms. Then comes "The Flowers of Punitaqui," after which he greets his Spanish-speaking
colleagues. In "New Year's Chorale for the Country in Darkness" he takes on the Chilean Government and then recalls
"The Great Ocean with his Rapa Nui":

Tepito-te-henua, navel of the great sea,
workshop of the sea, extinguished diadem.

The book closes with "I Am," in which he leaves his last testament, after looking once again at himself:

I leave my house by the seaside
in Isla Negra to the labor unions
of copper, coal and nitrate.
Let them rest here, those abused children
of my country, plundered by axes and traitors,
dispersed in its sacred blood,
consumed in volcanic tatters,

...I leave my old books, collected
in corners of the globe, venerated
in their majestic typography,
to the new poets of America,
to those who'll

one day weave tomorrow's meanings
on the raucous interrupted loom.

Finally, he shouts:

This book ends here.

...And this word will rise again,
perhaps in another time free of sorrow,
without the impure fibers that adhered
black vegetation in my song,
and my burning and starry heart
will flame again in the heights.
And so this book ends, here I leave
my Canto general written
on the run, singing beneath
the clandestine wings of my country.
Today, February 5, in this year
of 1949, in Chile, in "Godemar
de Chena," a few months before
I turned forty-five.

With this conclusion from François Villon, he ends the greatest volume in Latin American poetry. It is the epic of our
time, brushing with its curious wings all that is good and evil in the great land of our birth. There is room for nothing
but struggle. As with Araucana of his brilliant forbear, it is a continuous fight, and its caress is the clumsy caress of the
soldier, which is no less loving for being awkward, charged as it is with the power of the earth.

This page: "Goethe... whose multifaceted genius was crystallized in Faust." Sierra Maestra, Cuba, 1957.

Bolivia is the conclusion and the continuation of the journey undertaken by the young Ernesto almost 15 years previously.

The story of what occurred there has been recounted many times, with better or worse luck, with good or doubtful intentions, in words and images, from 1967 until today.

At the center is the memory of this "condottieri of the 20th century," with his surprising habit of being reborn at every turn in the path, that is, in history itself.

Che's Bolivian papers remain an essential part of that memory; it is exciting and instructive to find that we possess news, details, the heart of that postponed La Higuera story, thanks to the words that Ramón/Fernando/Mongo/Ernesto/Che left for us in his war diaries.

Through these notes we can follow the physical and spiritual traces of the guerrilla, know the details of his life during the campaign, the excitement of the ambushes, the tragedy of the unexpected deaths.

This man was consistent with the path Ernesto chose in his journey through Our America; consolidated in the heights of the Sierra Maestra; defined in his vocation as a nation builder; and profiled in international debates where his intelligence and integrity shone through.

He was also faithful to his vision and his vocation as a witness, determinedly analyzing others and himself to improve the world and its peoples.

We have included the evaluations, born from the tension and anguish of the war, Che wrote about two of his combatants, and the analysis of one of the first months of the guerrillas' life on Bolivian soil.

"A black day for me" carries the echo of the notes from his unfinished diary. The image of the "small, brave captain" reinforces the poetry which accompanied it in times of love and war. The books carried from pack to hiding place remind us of Che's willingness to understand and learn, as evidenced by the commentaries on his reading which have come to us from among his papers.

These are the keys to the one journey this book has tried to follow through photographs and manuscripts, chronicles and images, so we, too, can share the universal joys, the sadness which touches us, the hopes and dreams which these pages offer.

Here, both today and tomorrow. On Saint Guevara's Day, celebrated once on Peruvian territory, and while people are "capable of trembling with indignation each time an injustice is committed in the world" to be celebrated at any point of this yet unfinished journey.

—VC

14

"with the shield on my arm, the whole fantasy"

myarrivalwas uneventful...

November:
Analysis of the month

Everything has gone quite well. My arrival was uneventful. Half the people have arrived, also without incident, although with some delay. Ricardo's main collaborators have joined the struggle, come hell or high water. The general picture appears good in this remote region; everything indicates we shall be able to stay here practically as long as we wish.

The plans are to wait for the rest of the people, increase the number of Bolivians to at least 20, and begin operations. We still need to ascertain Monje's reaction and how Guevara's* people will conduct themselves.

* "Guevara" here refers to Moisés Guevara, the Bolivian miners' leader who subsequently joined the guerillas.

This page: Che as "Ramón Benítez," with Fidel Castro, heading to the Congo. Havana, Cuba, 1965.

the warm morning sunlight illuminates the scene...

(fragment   the   of   (eliseo   ))

your small dead body, brave captain...

(on   death)

January 10, 1967

Today I am on a surveillance mission in a beautiful place, and I lament the fact that I don't have a camera with me to take some photographs of this area. I am on a mountain which is just as picturesque as those I have seen in the movies. To my right, the river flows gently over large rocks, causing thunderous falls. Beyond the river begins a mountain range, towering and covered with dense vegetation, rising almost vertically from the stream to form a number of peaks. The summit of each one is covered in a thick mist, while further down the warm morning sun illuminates the scene and makes me interrupt my reading (I'm reading *The Charterhouse of Parma*) and remember those I love: my wife, Eleisito, Marisela and Renecito. I think of my mother, and the surprise she must have had when my father told her that I was fighting on the side of.. with P.

April 25, 1967

A black day. At around 10 a.m., Pombo returned from the lookout, warning that 30 soldiers were advancing on the little house...

Soon the army's advance unit appeared. To our surprise, it included three German shepherds and their guide. The animals were restless, but I did not think they would give us away. However, they continued advancing and I shot at the first dog, but missed. When I went after the guide, my M-2 jammed. Miguel shot the other dog, according to what I could see, although it could not be confirmed. No one else entered the ambush.

Intermittent firing began along the army's flank. When it stopped I sent Urbano to order the withdrawal, but he came back with the news that Rolando was wounded. They brought his lifeless body back a short time later, and he died as they began to give him plasma. A bullet had split open his thighbone and the entire nerve and vascular bundle; he bled to death before we could act.

We have lost the best man in the guerrilla unit, one of its pillars. He was a comrade of mine from the time when [in Cuba], barely a child, he served as messenger for Column No. 4, through the invasion, to this new revolutionary venture. Concerning his obscure and unheralded death, all that can be said, with eyes toward a hypothetical future that may come about, is: "The lustrous image of your small dead body, brave captain, extends into the immense unknown."

evaluationofrolando

Rolando 11/20/66

2/20/67 — three months: Very good; he hasn't carried out his role of political organizer, but he is a permanent example for the troops.

Dead, *4/25/67*, in the line of fire. An exemplary attitude, a first-rate example, has been extinguished; a pillar of the guerrilla forces has crumbled. He is worthy of a posthumous tribute which is greater than the importance he was given in life, where his modesty conspired against his outstanding nature.

Above: Bolivia, 1967.

a black day for me…

the end of fame (carlos puebla)

June 26, 1967

A black day for me. Everything seemed to be going peacefully as I sent five men to relieve those stationed on ambush at the Florida road. Suddenly shots were heard. We left rapidly on horseback and came across a strange spectacle: amid total silence, the bodies of four little soldiers were lying in the sun, on the sand by the river. We were unable to take their weapons since we did not know the enemy's position.

It was 5 p.m., and we were waiting for nightfall to recover the weapons. Miguel then sent word that the sound of cracking branches could be heard to his left. Antonio and Pacho went there, but I gave the order not to fire unless they could see something. Almost immediately gunfire broke out, which became generalized on both sides. I gave the order to withdraw, since we were at a disadvantage under these circumstances. The withdrawal was delayed and we received word of two wounded: Pombo in the leg and Tuma in the stomach.

We brought them rapidly to the house so we could operate on them with what we had. Pombo's wound is superficial, and will merely result in headaches for us due to his lack of mobility. Tuma's wound had destroyed his liver and he had suffered intestinal perforations. He died during the operation. With his death I have lost an inseparable comrade and companion over all the recent years. His loyalty was unwavering, and I feel his absence almost as if he were my own son. After he fell he asked that I be given his watch, and since they did not do so while he was being treated, he took it off and gave it to Arturo. Behind this gesture was the desire that it be given to the son whom he did not know, as I had done with the watches of many comrades who had died in the past. I shall carry it throughout the entire war. We loaded the body on to an animal and will bury it far from here.

evolution of fama

Tuma 11/7/66

2/7/67 — three months — perfect in his secondary role as my assistant.

5/7/67 — six months — Good. Had a period of depression, which was almost universal, but has overcome it.

Dead in combat 6/26/67. This is a considerable loss for the guerrilla forces, but especially for me as I now lose the most loyal of *compañeros*.

Right: Lookout, Ñancahuasú, Bolivia, 1967.

Not the reclining Christ, nor the anatomy class, nor the final chronological images overdone in so many publications and remembrances over the last few years... This book closes here, but the book of lived and future memory is truly opening; what we now call dreaming, ethics, invention or hope.

First, with his friends, listening or laughing.

Then, dressed for the occasion of the next adventure, ready to leave for other lands, in photographs published here for the first time.

Perhaps sharpening the humor of that phrase that originated his first journey: "This wandering around 'Our America with a Capital A' has changed me more than I believed."

Or temporarily taking his leave, as in that other phrase taken from his endless travels: "I leave you now with myself; the man I used to be..."

—VC

in imagery in memory

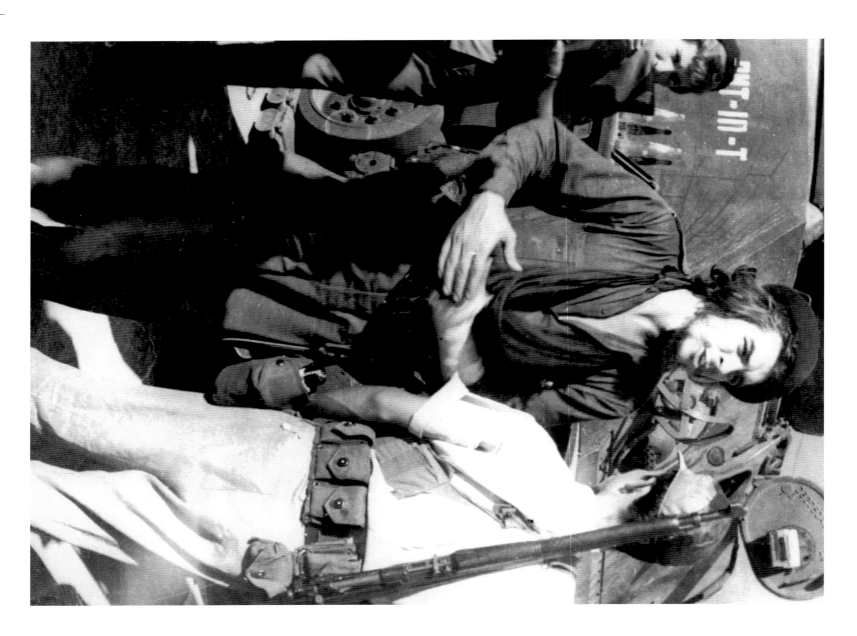

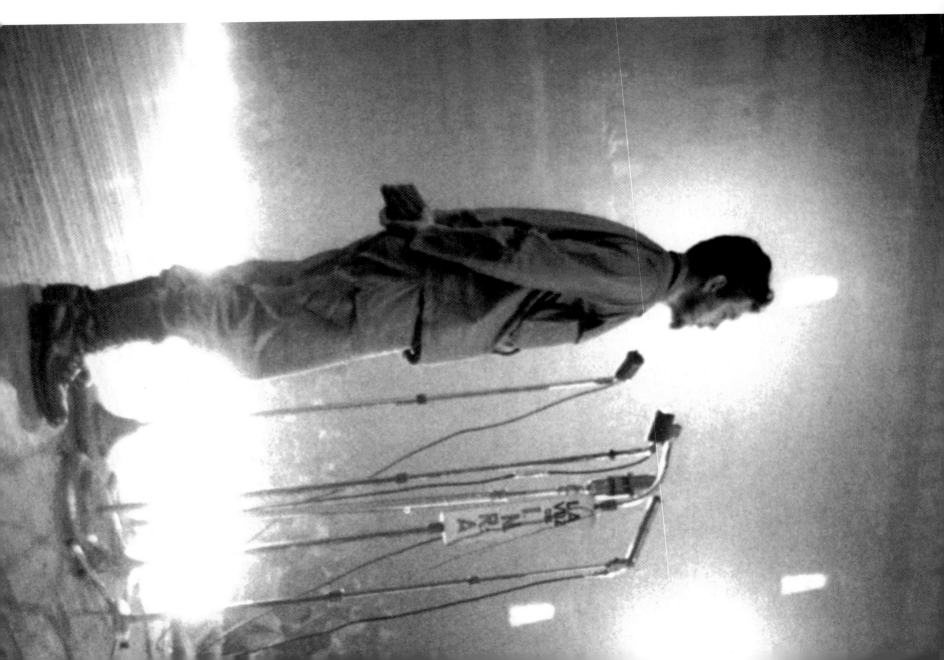

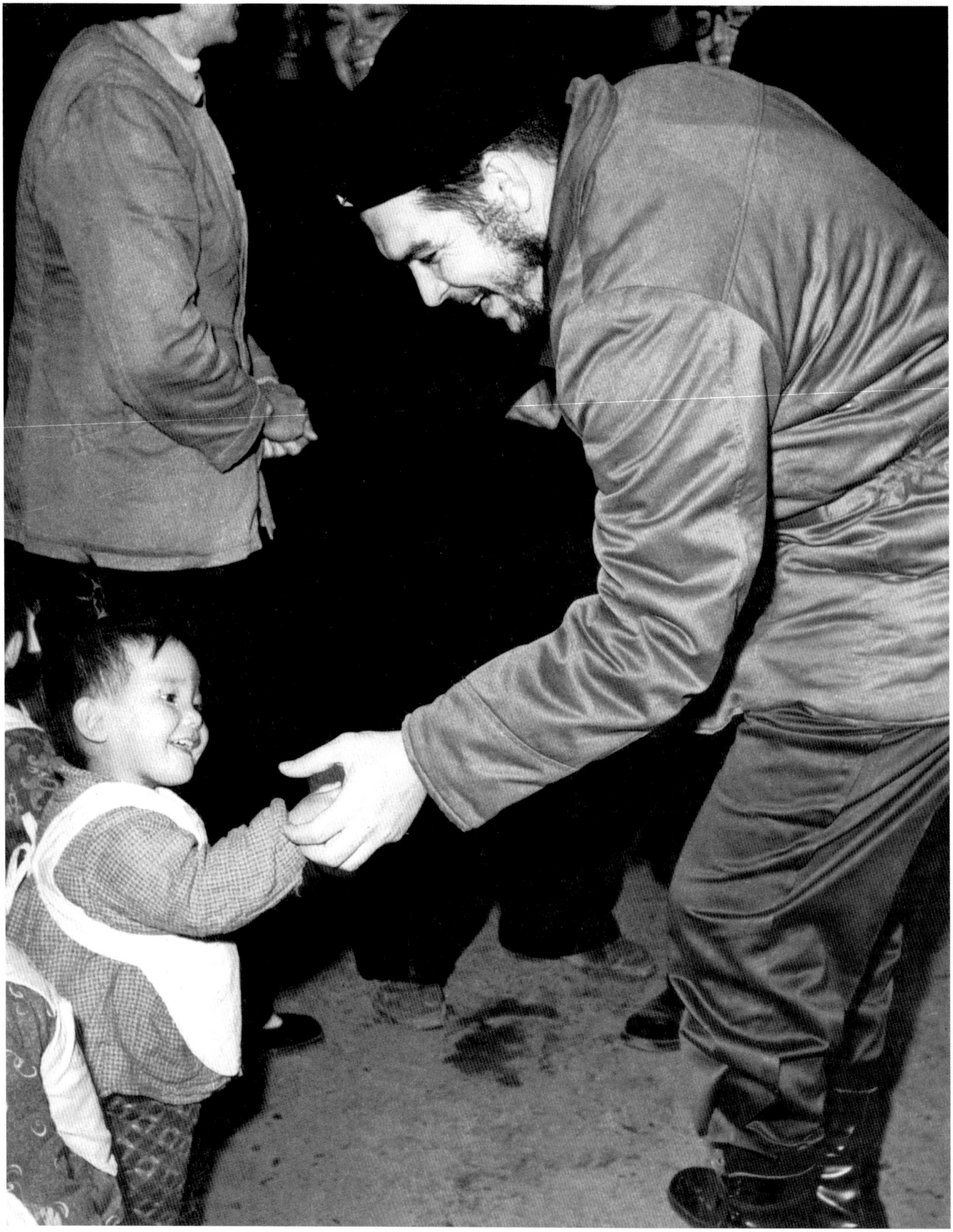

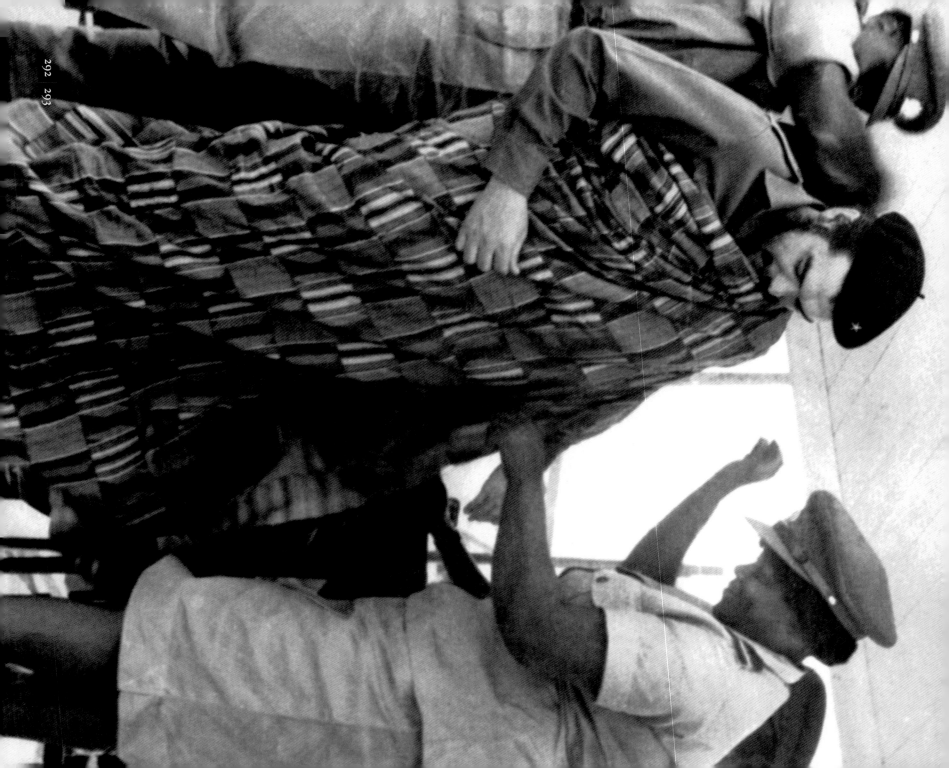

The Pablo de la Torriente Brau Center, founded in Havana in 1996, is an independent not-for-profit cultural institution. It has created programs and spaces for the dissemination of ideas and debate related to memory, oral history, testimony, plastic arts and Cuban Nueva Trova. It is inspired by the historical and literary legacy of Pablo de la Torriente Brau, and bases itself on new technologies and artistic creations.

maybe

::maybe is a creative collective based in Melbourne, Australia. With an in-depth literacy in visual language, enthusiastic creativity and social understanding, ::maybe aims to contribute intellectual art to an international audience. ::maybe offers visual and creative solutions, utilizing both traditional and new media in a fresh and stimulating manner. Their work is a cocktail of strong typography, rich imagery, radical ideas, cultural relevance and philosophy.

::maybe expects the impossible and accepts nothing less.

Che Guevara Studies Center

The Che Guevara Studies Center of Havana, Cuba, is the institution established to promote, both inside and outside Cuba, the thought, life and works of Ernesto Che Guevara, recognizing the extraordinary significance of his theory, praxis and ethical legacy — and their validity and timeliness in today's globalized world. The Center is located in the house where Che lived with his family until his final departure from Cuba.

Ocean Press

Ocean Press is an independent publisher with a unique list of books offering a radical global vision of politics and history, with a strong focus on Latin America. Our books are designed to capture the imagination of those who not only believe that another world is possible but who are actively working toward bringing that world into being. Our titles feature a series of readers by some renowned fighters for social justice from the Third World, including Che Guevara, Salvador Allende, José Martí and Fidel Castro.

We have recently initiated two series of books designed to nourish the "new activism" by providing vital information and inspiration from the past in inexpensive, accessible paperbacks for today. Published as Radical History and Rebel Lives, these mini-anthologies have been compiled from a rich seam of political writing, previously unavailable to non-academic readers. The selections sparkle with a contemporary relevance that reveal astonishing similarities between today's struggles and those that have gone before.

Ocean Press publishes several titles exposing the history and exploits of the CIA in Latin America and around the world. We also offer an expanding list of Spanish-language books.

www.oceanbooks.com.au

The Che Guevara Publishing Project

A series of books has been launched by Ocean Press and the Che Guevara Studies Center of Havana, with the objective of disseminating the works and ideas of Che Guevara — this most contemporary of radical role models.

Although perhaps best known as a guerrilla fighter, this multi-volume series will show Che Guevara as a profound thinker with a radical world view, who still strikes a chord with young rebels in every country today. Readers will be introduced to Che the political economist and philosopher, to Che the revolutionary humanist.

Some of these works have never before been published — such as Che's *Critical Notes on Political Economy*. Other works have only recently been uncovered, while many have been overlooked or available intermittently. A number of the books are thematic anthologies, such as *Latin America* — an exhaustive selection of Che's vision toward Latin America from 1950 to 1967.

All these works will be published in English and Spanish-language editions, discovering a Che who is more than an icon on a T-shirt or poster and restoring his cultural depth, his incisiveness, his irony and his passion.

New titles in the Che Guevara Publishing Project

Che Guevara Reader
Writings on Politics and Revolution

The Motorcycle Diaries
Notes on a Latin American Journey

Latin America
Awakening of a Continent

Global Justice
Liberation and Socialism

Our America and Theirs
Kennedy's Alliance for Progress

The Great Debate on Political Economy
A humanist approach to Marxist economics

Critical Notes on Political Economy
A critical analysis of the Soviet economic system

Socialism and Humanity in Cuba
A Classic Edition

Other Ocean Press titles about Che Guevara

Che: A Memoir by Fidel Castro
Edited by David Deutschmann

Che Guevara and the Latin American Revolutionary Movements
By Manuel "Barbarroja" Piñeiro

Che Guevara and the FBI
The U.S. Political Police Dossier on the Latin American Revolutionary
Edited by Michael Ratner and Michael Steven Smith